YOUNG STUDENTS

Learning Library

VOLUME 11

Inca–Klondike

WEEKLY READER BOOKS

MIDDLETOWN · CONNECTICUT

PHOTO CREDITS

A-Z BOTANICAL COLLECTION page 1348(top left). HEATHER ANGEL page 1279 (top left & center). BBC HULTON PICTURE LIBRARY page 1317(top right). BIOFOTOS page 1278(center left). BRITISH MUSEUM page 1258(bottom left); 1261(bottom right). BRITISH STEEL page 1304(top left). KRISTI BROWN page 1313(bottom left). RICHARD BRYANT page 1287(top right). CANADIAN INFORMATION SERVICE page 1367(top right). J. ALLAN CASH page 1267(top right); 1308(top left). MICHAEL CHINERY page 1278(top); 1279(bottom right); 1280(top left). COLUMBIA RECORDS page 1317(bottom right); 1325(top left). ARMANDO CURCIO EDITORE, SPA page 1248(top left); 1252(bottom left); 1260(top left); 1270(top); 1271(top); 1279(bottom left); 1303(bottom right); 1306(both pics); 1311(bottom right); 1316(bottom); 1318(center left); 1319(both pics); 1324(top right); 1325(top right); 1326(bottom); 1327(top right); 1329(top right); 1331(center left); 1339(top right); 1349(both pics). DRIGGS, NEW YORK page 1326(top left). EDITORIAL PHOTOCOLOR ARCHIVES page 1334(top right). FOTOMAS INDEX page 1320(top left). CLINTON E. FRANK FOR TRIFARI page 1334(bottom left). FREER GALLERY OF ART page 1333 (bottom left). PHILIP GRUSHKIN page 1336(bottom left). SONIA HALLIDAY page 1276(bottom left); 1305(top right); 1307(top right); 1309(bottom right); 1310(bottom left); 1329(bottom right); 1330(top right); 1341(bottom right). ROBERT HARDING page 1267(top right); 1300(bottom). HAWAII VISITORS BUREAU page 1351(bottom right). MICHAEL HOLFORD page 1247(bottom right); 1263(bottom right); 1322(top left). STATE OF INDIANA page 1257(center right). INDIANA DEPT. OF COMMERCE page 1255(top right); 1258(top left). IOWA DEVELOPMENT COMMISSION page 1298(top left). IRISH TOURIST BOARD page 1301(top right). ISRAEL TOURIST OFFICE page 1335(top center). ITN page 1343(top right). KC PUBLICATIONS page 1259(both pics). STATE OF KANSAS DEPT. OF ECONOMIC DEVELOPMENT page 1353(bottom right). DEPT. OF PUBLIC INFORMATION KENTUCKY page 1360(bottom left); 1362(both pics). KEYSTONE page 1358(top left). KUNST DIAS page 1331(bottom). LIBRARY OF CONGRESS page 1293(top left); 1338(both pics); 1339(bottom left); 1340(top left); 1370(top left). FLORENCE MALLET page 1269(top right). MANSELL COLLECTION page 1274(bottom left); 1275(top right); 1368(top right). BILL MAQUITTY page 1254(top left). DES MOINES CONVENTION AND VISITORS BUREAU page 1296(top left). MUSEO CORRER VENICE page 1311(top right). NBC page 1344(top left); 1357(center right). NATIONAL GALLERY OF ART, WASHINGTON, D.C. page 1311(bottom left); 1330(bottom left). NATIONAL MUSEET, BELGIUM page 1333(bottom right). NATIONAL PORTRAIT GALLERY, LONDON page 1357(top right); 1368(center left). PETER NEWARK'S WESTERN AMERICANA page 1274(top left); 1359(center right). DANIEL OCKO page 1302(top left). PENNSYLVANIA DEPT. OF COMMERCE page 1250(left). PHOTOSOURCE page 1366(center left). PICTORIAL PARADE page 1358(bottom center). POPPERFOTO page 1304(bottom right); 1310(top left); 1348(center left); 1364(bottom left). PRESS ASSOCIATION page 1369(top right). PUBLIC ARCHIVES OF CANADA page 1262(top left). SCALA page 1367(bottom right). SHARP ELECTRONICS page 1324(top left). SIEMENS page 1249(top right). SMITHSONIAN INSTITUTION page 1342(top left). SOLARFILMA page 1308(top right). SYNDICATION INT page 1290(top left). SYON HOUSE page 1286(top left). BRUCE F. TOURVILLE page 1273(center right). ULSTER MUSEUM page 1334(top left). UNION PACIFIC RAILWAY page 1264(bottom). UNITED NATIONS page 1259(both pics); 1291(bottom). UNITED STATES DEPT. OF AGRICULTURE page 1277(bottom right). M. VAUTIER page 1264(center top). VERVE RECORDS page 1325(center bottom). WASHINGTON CONVENTION & VISITORS BUREAU page 1249(bottom right). DAVID & JILL WRIGHT page 1363(top right). ZEFA page 1246; 1253(top & bottom right); 1254(bottom left); 1260(bottom right); 1264(center & right); 1268(bottom right); 1272(bottom); 1273(top right); 1282(bottom left); 1286(bottom left); 1291(top right); 1299(bottom); 1302(bottom left); 1305(center bottom); 1307(bottom right); 1314(top); 1344(bottom left); 1345(bottom right); 1352(center right); 1354(bottom right); 1355(top right); 1356(bottom left). ZIONIST ARCHIVES AND LIBRARY page 1336(top left).

Young Students Learning Library is a trademark of Field Publications.

Copyright © 1990, 1989, 1988, 1982, 1977 Field Publications; 1974, 1972 by Funk & Wagnalls, Inc. & Field Publications.

ISBN 0-8374-6041-7

CONTENTS

INCA When the Spanish conquistadors arrived in South America in the 1500's, they found a great Indian civilization. At its height, the Inca Empire covered an area that would stretch from Maine to South Carolina in the United States. The center of the empire was located in what is now Peru. The rest of the empire stretched across the western coast of South America in parts of present-day Argentina, Bolivia, Chile, and Ecuador. This land was inhabited by six to eight million Indians of various tribes. The capital of the empire, Cuzco, was a beautiful city of temples and palaces of stone and gold. The Incas ruled over this empire for more than four centuries.

The Inca Civilization A great network of stone roads connected all parts of the empire. Since there were no wheeled vehicles or horses, these roads were traveled by swift runners who provided an efficient communications system. The runners would memorize messages because the Incas had no writing system. Post houses were located along the roads for the runners, who worked in a relay system. Each person ran a few miles, then gave the message to a fresh runner. The relay system could cover up to 300 miles (500 km) a day. In times of war or during a rebellion of one of the conquered tribes, armies could travel quickly over these roads to all parts of the empire. Storehouses along the way contained provisions for the soldiers. There were also inns where travelers could stop and rest.

The Incas built sturdy suspension bridges over wide ravines and canyons. Some of these rope bridges are still being used. Other remarkable engineering achievements were vast temples, palaces, and fortresses of

◀ The Taj Mahal, built by Shah Jahan as a tomb for his beloved wife, is one of India's most magnificent monuments. (See INDIA.)

stone. The stones were carefully cut to enable them to fit together, since the Incas had no cement or other mortar. The stones were so well fitted that a knife blade could not be inserted between them. The Incas also built canals and aqueducts to bring water to their fields.

INCA LIFE. Most of the Incas were farmers. Their language was Quechua, which is still spoken today by the Indians of the Andes. A farmer and his family lived in a stone hut, which had only one windowless room. They had llamas and alpacas to carry light loads to markets. There they would trade their fresh vegetables for meat and cloth. They kept dogs as pets, and ducks and guinea pigs for food.

The Inca government believed that people worked for the state, but the state was responsible for the care of each of its citizens. Government officials taught the farmers how to build stone terracing, and how to fertilize, irrigate, and drain their fields. An irrigation ditch carried water from a nearby stream. The most important crops were corn and potatoes. A part of each grain harvest was stored in warehouses to be used in times of famine.

Some Incas were skilled metal workers. They made metal tools and weapons. They used gold to decorate their temples and palaces and to make beautiful jewelry. Ceramic pottery and woven cloth were also made by skilled craftworkers.

SCIENTIFIC ACHIEVEMENTS. The Inca astronomers charted the solar system and worked out the time for the planting and harvesting of crops. Most medicines were made from herbs or the organs of animals. These were boiled and put in the sick person's food. The Incas were the first to discover that quinine helped in the treatment of malaria.

The Inca number system was based on 10. Population figures and other important statistics were recorded on

▲ After the Spanish conquest, the last survivors of the mighty Inca empire took refuge in the isolated mountaintop town of Machu Picchu.

▼ A gold knife used in Inca ceremonies.

▲ *A decorative costume worn by an Inca warrior.*

The Incas were the first people to cultivate potatoes. They even invented a way of preserving them by freezing thin slices and then extracting the water. The same basic process is used today to make "instant" mashed potato.

During the time of the great Inca empire, the word "Inca" only referred to the nobility and those of royal blood.

quipus. A quipu is a long fiber rope with shorter ropes hanging from it. These hanging ropes were of different colors and could be tied into knots. A knot could stand for 1, 10, 100, or any multiple of 10. Using the quipu, the Incas managed to keep records not only of population figures and crop yields, but also of historical events and daily activities.

THE INCA GOVERNMENT. The Inca emperor was the supreme ruler. The people believed that he was descended from the sun god. In rank below the emperor were the royal family, nobles, government administrators, soldiers, craftworkers, farm laborers, and slaves taken from conquered tribes.

The entire empire was divided into four regions, or units. These regions were subdivided into various smaller regions, and the smallest unit was the farmland worked by a family. Government planners often moved and resettled whole populations for political and economic reasons. Government officials were in charge of each region, and the official of a small region would be under the supervision of the official of the next- largest region. These officials were responsible not only for the work done in their regions, but also for the well-being of every person under their management. This extremely efficient method of governing and the Inca communications system enabled the emperor and other officials in Cuzco to exercise firm control over all parts of the empire.

The Incas' system of law and justice was very stern but fair. If persons stole because they were greedy, they would be sentenced to a horrible death. But if persons stole because their families were hungry, they might just be fined a small amount, and the official who was responsible for their village would be punished.

The Fall of the Inca Empire This was the fabulous Indian empire that

Francisco Pizarro and his 177 soldiers saw in 1532. The Incas had never before seen white people, guns, or horses, and they thought the Spaniards were gods.

Pizarro returned their welcome by kidnapping the emperor, Atahualpa. The Incas offered a huge ransom of gold and silver for the return of their emperor. Pizarro took the ransom, and then ruthlessly killed Atahualpa. Without an emperor to lead them, the great Inca army was powerless against

▼ *By A.D. 1530 the Inca empire stretched for some 2,000 miles (3,200 km) north to south along the west coast of South America.*

the gunpowder of the Spaniards. In this manner, the Spaniards gained control of the Inca Empire. They allowed a new emperor to be crowned, but he no longer had any power. Most of the people were forced to work in the gold and silver mines for the Spaniards, and the farmlands soon fell into ruin. Many laborers died of overwork and starvation. The last Inca emperor was beheaded by the Spanish in 1571, and the Inca Empire disintegrated.

ALSO READ: ANCIENT CIVILIZATIONS; CIVILIZATION; CONQUISTADOR; INDIAN ART, AMERICAN; INDIANS, AMERICAN; PERU; PIZARRO, FRANCISCO.

INCUBATOR Chicken eggs will not hatch if they are not kept at a warm temperature of about 99 to 100 degrees F (37.2° to 37.7°C), for 18 to 21 days. In nature, a hen provides the warmth by sitting on the eggs in her nest. Large poultry farms that raise chickens to be sold in markets hatch the eggs in an incubator.

A large incubator may hold as many as 100,000 eggs. The eggs are kept warm by electric heaters. Special controls keep the air moist, so that the eggs will not become too dry. As the eggs develop into chicks, oxygen is used up. So fresh oxygen is pumped into the incubator.

The ancient Egyptians had incubators in which they could hatch a million eggs a year. Each incubator was a small, low building with double walls of dried mud. At one end of the building was a room in which a fire was kept burning.

Sometimes human babies are born *prematurely*—before they are fully developed. A premature baby can be kept in an incubator until it grows strong and healthy. An incubator for a baby is a crib with a special glass cover. The temperature inside the crib is kept at 80°F (26.7°C) and oxygen mixed with other gases is

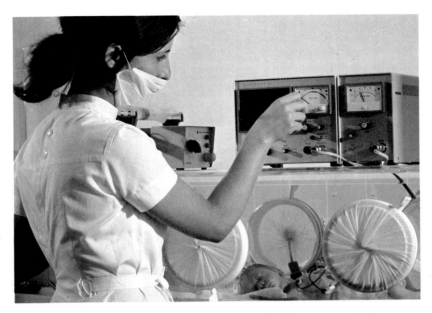

pumped into the incubator. A premature baby is very weak and catches serious diseases easily. The incubator protects the baby from germs and gives the baby a chance to grow strong.

ALSO READ: EGG, POULTRY, REPRODUCTION.

▲ *This premature baby was born before it was ready to live an independent life outside its mother's body. The incubator increases the baby's chance of survival.*

INDEPENDENCE DAY People all over the United States celebrate their country's "birthday" each year on the Fourth of July. This joyous holiday is called Independence Day because on that day, July 4, 1776, the Declaration of Independence was adopted by representatives of America's 13 original colonies. This declaration informed the world that the colonies, fighting for their freedom from Great Britain in the American Revolution (1775–1783), were now "free and independent states." On July 8, 1776, the first great celebration of this event took place in Philadelphia, Pennsylvania. Bells rang, cannon were fired, and band music filled the air as a grand parade marched down the main street. In the evening, the people enjoyed feasting, dancing, bonfires, and fireworks.

The custom of celebrating the anniversary of the beginning of the

▼ *A fireworks display at the Washington Monument is a traditional way of celebrating Independence Day in the nation's capital.*

It was on Independence Day, 1884, that the United States received the gift of the Statue of Liberty from the people of France.

▲ *A patriotic parade outside Independence Hall in Philadelphia celebrates America's birth of freedom.*

Before the British occupied Philadelphia during the Revolutionary War, the Liberty Bell was moved to Allentown, Pennsylvania. It was returned to Independence Hall when the British withdrew.

United States spread throughout the growing young country and all its territories and possessions. The Fourth of July became a red, white, and blue day of picnics and parades, games, athletic contests, and fireworks. Many towns and cities today have community festivities, ending the day with dazzling firework displays. The sizzling, hissing, ear-rattling explosions and the glorious flashes of color in the night sky make an exciting finish to Independence Day.

ALSO READ: AMERICAN REVOLUTION, DECLARATION OF INDEPENDENCE.

INDEPENDENCE HALL Some of the most important events in United States history took place in an old two-story, red-brick building in Philadelphia, Pennsylvania. Independence Hall was the meeting place of the Continental Congress from 1775 to 1781. George Washington was appointed commander in chief of the Continental Army there in 1775. The Declaration of Independence was adopted in the east room of the building on July 4, 1776. Four days later the famous Liberty Bell, then hanging in the tower of the hall, was rung to acclaim its adoption.

In 1787, the Constitutional Convention, which wrote the Constitution of the United States, met in Independence Hall. The hall was also the meeting place of the U.S. Supreme Court from 1789 to 1800.

Independence Hall was built between 1732 and about 1750. A wooden bell tower originally stood on top, but the present tower dates from 1828.

Independence Hall has since been restored to look exactly as it did in 1776. It is now a national historical museum. Visitors to the hall can see the original desk and chair used for signing the Declaration of Independence, portraits of most of the signers, colonial furniture, and many historical documents.

Independence Hall is part of Independence National Historical Park. This is a park covering four blocks in the heart of downtown Philadelphia. In 1948, Congress established the park to preserve the historical buildings and surroundings. They wanted visitors to see the buildings that played a part in the founding of the United States. The Liberty Bell is housed in a special exhibition building near Independence Hall.

ALSO READ: AMERICAN REVOLUTION, CONTINENTAL CONGRESS, DECLARATION OF INDEPENDENCE, LIBERTY BELL, PHILADELPHIA.

INDEX An index is a list, arranged in alphabetical order, of names, topics, and other factual matter to be found in a book, pamphlet, or other publication. An index is placed at the end of the publication. Each entry in the index contains the number of the page, section, or chapter in which the information appears. Most factual books have indexes.

A telephone book is a kind of index, listing in alphabetical order the names, addresses, and telephone numbers of people in a particular area

▼ *A section taken from the Index at the end of an encyclopedia showing how the entries are set out.*

who have telephones. Dictionaries and encyclopedias are indexes to language and to areas of human knowledge and the world.

■ **LEARN BY DOING**

Let's say you have a book about American Indians, and you want to find information about the famous Apache chief, Cochise. You first look up "Cochise" in the index section at the back of the book. When you find his name, make a note of the page numbers that are listed after his name. When you read those pages, you will find the information you need. If you use the index, you do not have to read through the whole book to find the special information you want.

Some indexes, such as encyclopedia indexes, are long enough to fill a whole book. The index for this encyclopedia does not fill an entire book, but it fills much of the last volume. Try locating an article about the composer, Ludwig van Beethoven, by using this index. First look up Beethoven's name. Be sure to look under B for "Beethoven," not L for "Ludwig." People are listed in an index by their last names. Beside Beethoven's name you can see two kinds of numbers. The first number tells you the volume (book) number. The second set of numbers gives you the pages on which the article about Beethoven can be found. Look through the volumes and find the one

listed for Beethoven. Is it volume 2 or 3? Now locate the pages that have information about Beethoven. Did you find it? ■

What happens if you want to look up something in a magazine? Magazines do not have indexes at the end of every issue, but every library has copies of the *Reader's Guide to Periodical Literature*. The *Reader's Guide* is an index that lists articles from almost all magazines.

Indexes are not always in books. Card files are a kind of index. The card or computer catalog in a library is an index of all the books in that library. Many business firms keep indexes, or *inventories*, that show what items are in their storerooms. Today these are often computerized. Computers are a new form of index. A computer can collect and organize information quickly.

ALSO READ: BIBLIOGRAPHY, CATALOG, LIBRARY, REFERENCE BOOK.

INDIA   The republic of India is the seventh largest country in the world. It is about one-third the size of the United States, but has more than three times as many people as the United States does. China is the only country whose population is larger than India's. Overcrowding becomes worse in India each year because the population increases rapidly.

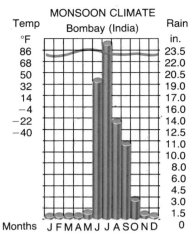
MONSOON CLIMATE
Bombay (India)

▲ *This graph shows India's monsoon climate. The rainy or monsoon season begins in June.*

People marry younger in India than in any other country. The average marrying age for males is 20; for females it is younger still at 14½.

INDIA

Capital City: New Delhi (273,000 people).
Area: 1,269,346 square miles (3,287,352 sq. km).
Population: 834,000,000.
Government: Republic.
Natural Resources: Bauxite, chromite, coal, copper, gold, iron ore, manganese.
Export Products: Textiles and clothing, tea, fish, farm products, machinery.
Unit of Money: Rupee.
Official Languages: Hindi, English.

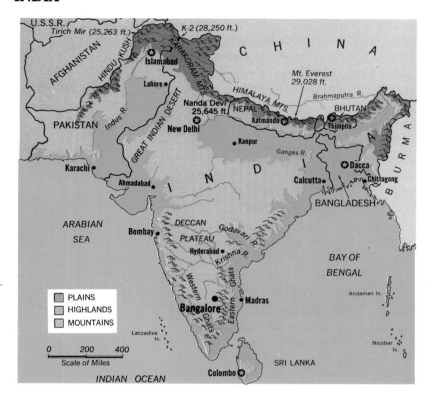

▲ *A woman of the province of Bihar, India. Her forehead is marked with a powder to show her religious belief.*

Geography and Climate India is called a *subcontinent* because its land area juts away from the Asian mainland into the Indian Ocean. The giant Himalayan Mountains stand along India's northern border with China, Nepal, and Bhutan. Nanda Devi, India's tallest mountain, 25,645 feet (7,817 m) high, is located there. Pakistan lies to the west of India, and Bangladesh and Burma are to the east. Three great rivers, the Indus, Ganges, and Brahmaputra, are supplied by Himalayan snows and glaciers. A wide plain lies south of the Himalayas, stretching between the Arabian Sea on the west and the Bay of Bengal on the east. The soil here is very fertile. The Deccan plateau lies south of this plain. It is separated from the coasts by mountains, called the Eastern Ghats and the Western Ghats.

Throughout much of India, the year is divided into three distinct seasons. The first season lasts from December to March. It is cool and dry, and the winds blow from the northeast across the Asian mainland. The second season, during April and May, is hot and dry. The third season, beginning in June, is rainy. This is the time of the *monsoon*, when strong winds bring heavy rain.

Natural Resources Rice, one of India's main crops, is grown in the Ganges River valley, along the coasts, and near rivers in the southern part of the country. Wheat, corn, and barley are raised in the northern part of India. Tea shrubs are grown in the moist, northeastern region called Assam. Cotton is grown in the drier southern and central areas. Jute is raised for its fiber, which is used in making rope and sacks. Rubber, pepper, and coffee are grown on plantations. Cashew nuts, coconuts, bananas, and citrus fruits are also raised. India has large deposits of valuable minerals, including high-grade iron ore, coal, mica, gypsum, manganese, chromite, salt, and oil. India's dense forests contain valuable woods, such as sandalwood, ebony, teak, and bamboo.

India's wildlife is varied—over 500 species of mammals. Indians value the elephant for its ability to do heavy work, such as lumbering. The tigers of India, especially the Bengal tigers,

▼ *These Indian women are picking tea, an important crop. They put the leaves in baskets slung from their heads.*

are known all over the world for the beautiful colors of their coats. *Maharajahs* (princes) of India hunted this prized animal for sport, as did the British. Fur merchants also hunted tigers, and now these animals are in danger of extinction. The government has established wildlife sanctuaries in Assam, Karnataka (formerly Mysore), Madras, and other places. These sanctuaries have been set up to preserve the lives of these animals, and no hunting is allowed.

People India is made up of various regions. The people in each region follow their own customs. They have their own ways of dressing and have developed their own styles of music and dancing. They even have their own languages. In 1956, the Indian government rearranged the state boundaries so that most of the people who speak the same language now live in the same state.

India has been called a nation of villages, because most of the people live in small communities. Village life is very important. India is primarily an agricultural nation, and the farm workers must produce enough food to feed India's huge population. Even with the many food products grown in India, the people often go hungry. When there is not enough rainfall, crops do not grow. Many Indians will not eat beef because of their religious belief that the cow is a sacred animal. In order to feed the people, India must import some of its food. Villagers in India are also employed in *cottage industries* where they work at home or in small workshops. Cottage industrial workers process food and make cloth and handicrafts.

Twelve cities in India have populations of more than one million persons. They are Calcutta, Bombay, Delhi, Madras, Bangalore, Hyderabad, Ahmadabad, Kanpur, Pune, Nagpur, Lucknow, and Jaipur. Calcutta, the largest city, has more than nine million persons living in

and around it. Madras has large textile mills and is noted for cotton cloth, called *madras*. City workers are employed in large factories where iron and steel, as well as machinery and fertilizer, are manufactured. Thousands of people have come to India's large cities from the country, hoping to find work. The cities now contain vast numbers of unemployed poor who have no food and live in the streets, because there is no place to house them.

Most of India's population lives along the three main river systems—the Indus, Ganges, and Brahmaputra. The Ganges is a holy river for the Hindus. Sacred shrines and temples line its banks. The great majority of Indians are either Hindu or Muslim, a few are Christian, and a few are Buddhist.

History Indian civilization is about 5,000 years old. Almost 2,500 years before the birth of Christ, a group of people, called Aryans, moved into the Indus River valley from the northwest. They gradually took over most of the northern area of India. Little is known about the people who lived in India before the Aryans came. Perhaps the original settlers were the Dravidians who live in southern India today. They are usually shorter and have somewhat darker skins than the people living in the north.

▲ *A market in the holy city of Varanasi (formerly Benares), India.*

▼ *A movie theater in the busy city of New Delhi. Movies are very popular in India, which has a thriving movie industry.*

▲ *The earliest Indian civilizations grew up along the Indus River. This carved stone head came from Mohenjo-Daro, the ruins of a 3,500-year-old city now in Pakistan.*

▼ *The stupa at Sanchi is one of the most famous Buddhist monuments in India. It was built by the Emperor Ashoka in the 200's B.C. and later enlarged.*

When the Aryans arrived in the north, the Dravidians moved to the south. The Aryans created a highly developed civilization. They raised crops and worked with metal tools. Two great religions, Buddhism and Hinduism, developed in India. Hinduism began about 3,000 years ago. Buddhism began in the 500's B.C. and spread to other Asian lands. In 326 B.C., a Greek army, led by Alexander the Great, invaded the Indus River valley region, but did not greatly affect the Aryan civilization. After the Greek invasion, the Aryan people united under Chandragupta, a native Indian ruler, and gained control of most of the country. Chandragupta was the first king of the Maurya dynasty. This *dynasty* (series of rulers belonging to the same family) lasted until 200 B.C. The greatest Mauryan emperor, Asoka, became a Buddhist and helped to spread that religion throughout the land.

Various dynasties held power during the next 300 to 400 years. The Sunga dynasty lasted the longest of these, ruling for more than 100 years. During the Sunga reign, Hinduism replaced Buddhism and again became the main religion. the Hindu *caste system* became widespread. The population was divided into religious classes (castes). Persons, when they were born, belonged to the caste of their parents. Throughout their life, they could associate with and marry only people who belonged to the same caste as they did. The caste system tended to keep people apart, which may be one of the reasons that India was so long in becoming a really unified nation. The caste system is now discouraged, but many Indians still practice and believe it.

Muslims from the Middle East came to India in the A.D. 700's and set up trading colonies there. With them they brought their faith, Islam. By the twelfth century, Muslim Turks had conquered all of the Ganges River valley east of Bengal. In 1398, the Mongol conqueror, Tamerlane, entered the country and captured the city of Delhi. For the next hundred years or so, India was an area of many small kingdoms. Then in 1526, Babur, a Muslim and a descendant of Tamerlane, conquered most of the Indian mainland, proclaimed himself emperor, and founded the Mogul dynasty. This dynasty, under the emperors Akbar, Jahangir, and Shah Jahan, encouraged learning, the sciences, and the arts. One of the most beautiful buildings in the world, the Taj Mahal, was built by Shah Jahan.

In the late 1400's Europeans began searching for new places with which to trade. The Portuguese explorer, Vasco da Gama, discovered a sea route to India in 1498. The Portuguese, Dutch, British, and French all battled for control of the Indian trade. England finally dominated the Indian trade in the 1700's, forming the British East India Company. The Mogul empire collapsed, and the British ruled India as a colony for nearly 200 years under the administrative control started by Robert Clive, called Clive of India.

India in the Twentieth Century
The Indian people began seeking independence in the late 1800's. In the

1920's, Mohandas (Mahatma) Ghandi became head of the independence movement. He started his civil disobedience campaign of nonviolence in which people peacefully refused to obey British laws. They boycotted elections, schools, and courts, and refused to buy British goods. The British could not rule under such conditions. In 1947, Britain gave up its power in India. Shortly afterward, the regions of India that were mostly Muslim formed the independent nation of Pakistan.

Since then, hostility and outbreaks of fighting have occurred between India and Pakistan. They fought for two years over the territory of Kashmir. After the ceasefire in January 1949, each nation was left in control of about half the territory. In 1971, India and Pakistan began fighting over who would rule East Pakistan. The Indians defeated the Pakistani army and made it possible for the people of East Pakistan to establish the new nation of Bangladesh.

India has been a member of the Commonwealth of Nations since 1950. Jawaharlal Nehru was the first prime minister, ruling from 1947 until his death in 1964. His daughter, Indira Gandhi, held that position from 1966 to 1977, when she was defeated in a general election. She was again elected prime minister in 1980, but she was assassinated in 1984. Her son, Rajiv Gandhi, took over as prime minister but was defeated in the 1989 election.

ALSO READ: ASIA; BUDDHISM; EAST INDIA COMPANY; GANDHI, INDIRA; GANDHI, MAHATMA; HINDUISM; MONSOON; NEHRU, JAWAHARLAL; PAKISTAN.

INDIANA People from Indiana are often called *Hoosiers*. It is not certain where this word came from. It may have come from the question "Who's yer?" that pioneers asked when a newcomer arrived in the state. Or it may have come from the name of a canal builder, Samuel Hoosier, who lived about 150 years ago. Hoosier hired Indiana men rather than those from other states. He said they worked the best.

Among the well-known Hoosiers are the poet James Whitcomb Riley, and the novelists Booth Tarkington and Theodore Dreiser. The songwriter Cole Porter was a Hoosier, too, as were Presidents Benjamin and William Henry Harrison.

The Land and Climate Indiana lies in the plains that curve south around the Great Lakes. To the north are Lake Michigan and the state of Michigan. Illinois is on the west. Ohio is on the east. The Ohio River forms the state's southern boundary with Kentucky.

Most of Indiana is in the basin of the Wabash River. Part of this basin is the valley of the White River, which flows into the Wabash. The soil here is very fertile.

When the early settlers came, most of the state was covered with woods of oak and hickory. The rest was prairie grassland. Today, crops grow where grass used to wave in the wind, and much of the forest has been cut down. Indiana now has several big cities, but fields, meadows, and woods cover 85 percent of its area.

Indiana has two valuable resources under its soil. One is coal; the other, stone. You may have heard of Indiana limestone. It is used all over the country in the construction of buildings.

Indiana summers are hot, but winds from Lake Michigan keep the heat in the northern sections from being unpleasant. Winters can be very cold. Rainfall is plentiful in Indiana. The state lies where cold air from the north meets warm, moist air from the Gulf of Mexico. The warm air is chilled by the cold. Once the air is cooled it cannot hold so much moisture, so rain falls.

▲ *An old fashioned general store in Billie Creek, Indiana, is a meeting place for young and old.*

The famous Indianapolis 500 automobile race takes place every year on the Saturday before Memorial Day. More than 300,000 people attend the race. The first "500" took place in 1911 and the winning car averaged 74.58 miles per hour (120 km/hr). The race is called the "500" because the first driver to complete 200 laps of the 2½-mile (4 km) track—a distance of 500 miles (805 km)—wins.

Corydon became Indiana's first state capital in 1813. Indianapolis became the permanent capital in 1825.

When the Civil War broke out, Indiana offered many more volunteers to the Union than could be accepted. About 100,000 men from Indiana served in the Union forces.

History *Indiana* means "Land of the Indians." Indians lived in the region long before white people came. They made copper ornaments and built great earthen mounds as burial places or as bases for their temples. No one knows what happened to the ancient mound-building Indians. When white people came to Indiana, other tribes were living there. The principal tribe was the Miami. During the 1600's and 1700's, tribes from the East moved into Indiana as Europeans took their lands along the Atlantic coast. French fur traders and Catholic priests were the first white persons to come to the Indiana region. The oldest town, established by the French, is Vincennes, located on the Wabash River. It was founded in the 1730's.

France lost the French and Indian War in 1763, and Great Britain took control of the French-held lands around the Great Lakes. In 1776, the British lost the region south of the lakes in the American Revolution. Virginia riflemen, led by Colonel George Rogers Clark, took Vincennes and other fortified places.

By the early 1800's, many American settlers had come into the Great Lakes region. Some Indian chiefs tried to hold onto what was left of their land. Tecumseh, a Shawnee chief, united a number of tribes. His brother, who was called "the Prophet," helped him. The brothers talked with William Henry Harrison, governor of the Indiana Territory. They asked him not to allow white settlers to take over more land without the consent of the united tribes. They also asked him to give back some of the land that had been bought from the Indians. Governor Harrison would not agree. He moved troops toward the Prophet's town near the Tippecanoe River. Tecumseh was away at the time. The Prophet led his warriors in an attack, but they were defeated at the battle of Tippecanoe in 1811. William Henry Harrison later became the ninth President of the United States.

After the War of 1812, nearly all the Indians of Indiana were forced to move westward, as white settlers arrived in large numbers. Indiana was made a state in 1816.

The Civil War brought serious problems to Indiana. As a northern state, Indiana backed the Union, but many of its citizens were originally from the South and sided with the Confederacy. The people of the state were divided by the quarrel during and after the war.

Indiana's coal brought wealth to the state. Coal was used in making steel. It was burned by the steam engines that ran factory machines, pulled trains, and turned the paddle wheels of boats. Luckily for Indiana's business executives and farmers, millions of people needed farm and factory equipment. Indiana could produce huge quantities of both. It became a manufacturing state as well as an agricultural state.

Indiana's central location and its trade made transportation very important to the state. Railroads, high-

▼ *Cows graze peacefully on the rich grass of Indiana's fertile central plain. Agriculture and manufacturing are both important industries for the state.*

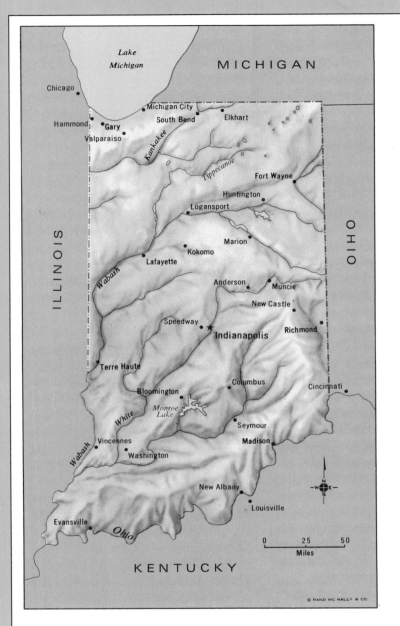

Lake Michigan

MICHIGAN

Chicago

Michigan City

Hammond · Gary
Valparaiso

South Bend

Elkhart

Kankakee

Tippecanoe

Fort Wayne

Huntington

Logansport

Marion

Kokomo

Lafayette

Anderson · Muncie

New Castle

Speedway ★

Indianapolis

Richmond

Terre Haute

Bloomington

Columbus

Cincinnati

Monroe Lake

Seymour

White

Madison

Vincennes

Washington

Wabash

New Albany

Louisville

Evansville

Ohio

KENTUCKY

ILLINOIS

OHIO

N W E S

0   25   50
Miles

© RAND MC NALLY & CO.

INDIANA

Capital and largest city
Indianapolis (710,000 people) (12th largest city in U.S.)

Area
36,291 square miles (93,986 sq. km)
Rank: 38th

Population
5,556,000 people   Rank: 14th

Statehood
December 11, 1816 (19th state admitted)

Principal river
Wabash River

Highest point
1,240 feet (378 m), close to the Ohio border

Motto
Crossroads of America

Song
"On the Banks of the Wabash, Far Away"

Famous people
Charles and Mary Beard, Hoagy Carmichael, Theodore Dreiser, Cole Porter, Ernie Pyle, Booth Tarkington.

▲ *This fine example of a covered bridge is one of the picturesque sights of rural Indiana.*

STATE EMBLEMS

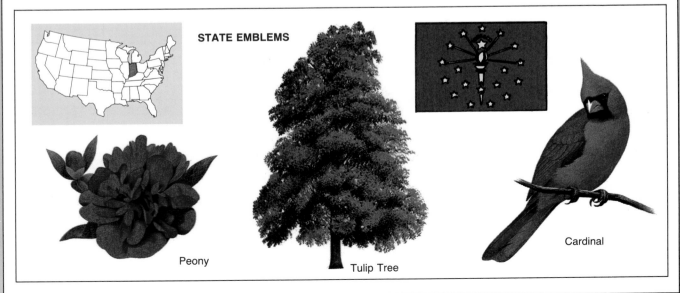

Peony

Tulip Tree

Cardinal

▲ *Indiana's first territorial capitol in Corydon.*

▲ *A Maya carving of about A.D. 709 from Central America. Maya artists decorated the great pyramid temples and palaces of their religious centers.*

ways, and airlines serve the state well. Since the opening of the Port of Indiana at Burns Harbor on Lake Michigan in 1970, Indiana has had rapid economic growth. Large ocean-going freighters and other ships coming from the St. Lawrence Seaway dock, unload, and take on cargoes there.

Hoosiers at Work Indianapolis is the largest manufacturing center in the state. Fort Wayne, Gary, Evansville, Kokomo, Muncie, and South Bend are important manufacturing cities, too. All together, Indiana turns out billions of dollars' worth of factory equipment and products every year. Machinery is first in value. Metals—mostly iron and steel—come next. The city of Gary is one of the greatest steel-producing centers in the world. Motor vehicles and other transportation equipment are made in Indiana's factories.

Indiana is an important agricultural state. Farmers grow corn (the state's main crop), soybeans, wheat, vegetables, and fruits. Much corn and other grain crops are fed to hogs and cattle, two valuable livestock products in Indiana. Many sheep, horses, and poultry are also raised in the state.

Indiana's beautiful open country brings many tourists. They come to see the ancient Indian mounds in Mounds State Park and the beautiful rolling sand dunes in Indiana Dunes State Park along Lake Michigan. Two large underground caves near Corydon, in the southern part of the state, attract thousands of visitors.

ALSO READ: CLARK, GEORGE ROGERS; FRENCH AND INDIAN WAR; GREAT LAKES; HARRISON, BENJAMIN; HARRISON, WILLIAM HENRY; RILEY, JAMES WHITCOMB; TECUMSEH; WAR OF 1812.

INDIAN ART, AMERICAN The American Indians have enriched North and South America with many

▲ *A page from a Mixtec document. The Mixtecs were conquered by the Aztecs shortly before the arrival of the Spanish.*

arts of great beauty. Museums display the sculpture, metalwork, and ceramics of Indians who lived a thousand years ago. After the coming of the white settlers, Indian skills blended with those of the newcomers to make beautiful art.

One of the earliest Indian skills was basket making. When a tribe of hunters settled down in one place for a while, the women would often weave baskets from certain grasses or willow shoots. Perhaps a nearby tree had bark or seed pods that produced certain dyes. A basket maker knew how to gather these grasses and dry them, and how to make dyes to color the grasses.

Even today many tribes of Indians make baskets. Some types of baskets are used in tribal ceremonies, while others are used for carrying or storing foods. Some tightly woven ones can even hold water! Hopi Indians of the Southwest weave coiled plaques (mats) to give as prizes to winners of foot races. Baskets have been used by some Indians as a way of paying someone for work.

Pottery making (ceramics) is an Indian skill of long standing in the Americas. Pottery breaks easily, but it lasts a long time. Archeologists have dug up pottery (much of it broken) from many ancient Indian cultures in the Americas. Each tribe or region had its own artists who painted pottery in a particular way. Archeologists can tell one culture from another by the style of the pottery they find. American Indians never used a potter's wheel. Instead, they made coils of clay, stacking them and shaping them to make bowls, plates, and other pottery shapes. Dyes in natural earth colors were used to paint pottery.

Among some Indian cultures pottery making became a very highly developed art, with complicated designs and painting techniques handed down through generations. This was true about a thousand years ago in the region of Veraguas, in what is now the republic of Panama. Elaborate designs of jaguars, crocodiles, frogs, and other wildlife are painted in many colors on Veraguas ceramics.

It was only a step from making useful clay pots and plates to making little clay figures—the beginning of sculpture among American Indians. Small clay figures were being made soon after 1500 B.C. in various parts of Mexico and Guatemala. An amazing amount of information about ancient Indian life has been learned from studying these small figurines. Some are holding babies, others are costumed as priests, dancers and even ball players.

From small ceramic figures, sculptors soon began creating very large pieces. Huge stone heads, some nearly 8 feet (2.4 m) high, were carved from stone by the Olmec people in Mexico. The first city culture of American Indians developed in the A.D. 200's in the center of Mexico, not far from where Mexico City is today. Here the great pyramids and temples of Teotihuacán were built. Sculp-

tured heads of the Plumed Serpent, Quetzalcoatl, and of Tlaloc, the rain god, decorate the temple of Quetzalcoatl that has been excavated there. A few hundred years later, sculpture decorated the great Mayan cities, such as Tikal in Guatemala. Huge temples were built by the Maya, and decorated with *stelae*, richly carved, upraised slabs of stone. Many stelae are covered with the hieroglyphics (picture language) of the Maya, as well as with sculptured figures and ornamental designs.

The Indians before Columbus also did some sculpture in silver, gold, copper, and tin. Sometimes copper and gold were melted together in an alloy. Indians in Bolivia melted tin and copper to form bronze. Gold figures of frogs, eagles, and sharks have been found in Central America and as far south as Peru.

The totem pole of the Pacific Coast Indians in the United States and Canada is a kind of sculpture. It was probably developed after the coming of the white settlers, but some people think that the idea of the totem could have been brought to the area by visitors from the South Pacific islands. The totem is rather like the sculpture done by primitive people in the South Pacific.

Indians of the southwestern United States make much silver jewelry, decorated with turquoise, a gemstone. Silver working was not known to these Indians until the Spanish came. After learning the craft from the Spanish, the Indians used their own tribal designs in making jewelry and became expert silversmiths.

Weaving was done by some tribes. The Incas of Peru wove the wool of

▲ *The Navaho Indians are widely known for their fine rug weaving. The rugs are made from handspun yarn, which gives them great strength and durability.*

▼ *The Papago Indians of southern Arizona weave more fine baskets than any other people in the United States. This collection demonstrates the skill and beauty of their work.*

▲ *An earthenware vase with a handle in the shape of an animal. It is a fine example of pottery made by the pre-Columbian High Plains Indians of Bolivia.*

the llama, alpaca, guanaco, and vicuña. The Pacific Northwest Indians wove blankets of goat hair mixed with a kind of cedar bark. The rugs woven by the Navaho Indians in the southwestern United States are well known. The Navaho began weaving their rugs after the Spanish brought sheep to the New World. Weaving continues to be a very important craft among the Indians in Guatemala.

Today, some Indians are doing paintings on paper and canvas, but this is a new art to them. Indians have painted for many hundreds of years, but they did their painting on pottery, wood, stone, hides, and on the walls of special buildings. The Navaho Indians did sand paintings, using colored sands, as part of their religious ceremonies. Some tribes painted designs on their tipis (teepees). Paints were made from earth colors, or from dyes gotten from seeds, berries, and the bark of certain trees.

Many Indians made beads from seashells. The beads were used on jewelry. Some inland tribes would journey great distances to the seashore to get shells for this purpose. Algonquian-speaking Indians on the Atlantic coast called their beads *wampum*. At one time these beads were used as money.

Many Indian crafts and arts died out when the white people changed the tribal ways of life. Today, many tribes throughout the Americas are trying to bring back their arts.

ALSO READ: AZTEC INDIANS; INDIANS, AMERICAN; MAYA; TOTEM.

INDIAN OCEAN The Indian Ocean is the third largest ocean in the world. Only the Atlantic and Pacific are bigger. The Indian Ocean touches four continents. Africa is on the west. Asia is the north boundary. In the south and east are Antarctica and Australia respectively.

Important trade routes cross the northern part of the Indian Ocean. Ships from the Pacific travel across the ocean to reach the Suez Canal and Europe. When the canal is closed, ships must sail around Africa to the Atlantic Ocean. Oil supertankers ply the ocean between the Arab nations of the Persian Gulf and other nations.

The Indian Ocean is more than 4,000 miles (6,400 km) wide at the equator and extends more than 6,000 miles (9,600 km) from north to south. At its deepest point, in the Java Trench, it is 25,344 feet (7,725 m)—almost 5 miles (8 km)—deep.

Several important islands are located in the Indian Ocean. The largest ones are Madagascar, near Africa, and Sri Lanka, just off the tip of

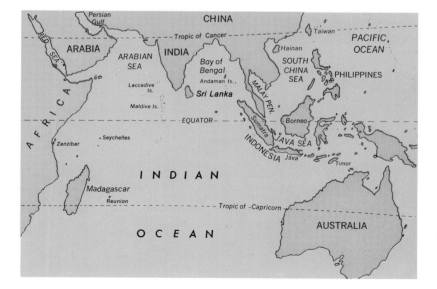

▼ *The Seychelles are a small group of beautiful tropical islands in the Indian Ocean.*

India. Other islands include the Seychelles, which attract many tourists because of the warm weather.

Much of southeast Asia gets its seasonal weather from the Indian Ocean. Strong winds from the ocean, called *monsoons*, bring moisture deep inland each summer. This seasonal rainfall is needed for crops.

ALSO READ: OCEAN, WEATHER.

INDIANS, AMERICAN (Native Americans)

When Christopher Columbus "discovered" the New World in 1492, he thought he had reached Asia and had landed in the East Indies. He called the people he found in this new land "Indians." The ancestors of these Native Americans had come from Asia many, many years before Columbus saw them.

Thousands of years ago, the Earth was in an ice age. People who lived in northeastern Asia found their homeland growing colder and colder. *Glaciers* (huge sheets of ice) were spreading over the land, and the animals people hunted for food were being forced away. The people also had to move, to stay near the animals. Some groups of people crossed from Asia to North America across a narrow passage now called the Bering Strait. This strait is part of the Pacific Ocean and separates northeastern Asia from Alaska. Thousands of years ago, however, the area may have been a thick sheet of ice or even a grassy plain. So groups of people—ancestors of American Indians—crossed this "land bridge" to Alaska. All this happened over 40,000 years ago. Some scientists think it may have happened even earlier. These people slowly traveled east and south, searching for areas where hunting was good. Their children and all those who came after them continued to spread throughout the New World. Geographers think that it may have taken as long as 25,000 years from the time the first

groups crossed the strait until their descendants reached the southern tip of South America and settled there.

The Indians are members of the Mongoloid race, and their physical characteristics are related to those of the Asian people of Japan and China. Most Indians do not have yellowish skin or the "slanted" eyes that many Asian people have. Some have coppery, or reddish brown, skin. But—like the people of Japan and other countries of the Far East—Indians usually have high cheekbones and straight black hair.

The Indians and White People Colonists came from England, France, and other European countries to America during the 1600's. Small towns were built, and the towns grew larger as more and more colonists arrived. Groups of settlers moved across the land, looking for good places to set up a town, a trading post, or a farm. As the settlers traveled, they often met Indians. At first, the meetings were friendly. The Indians were almost always curious about white people, and they were generous, too. Indians often gave the white people food and shelter. Indians taught white settlers to grow many important crops, including corn, peanuts, pumpkins, squash, and tobacco.

The Indians' way of life was very different from that of the white settlers. It is important to understand the Indians' beliefs and customs because the differences between Indians and whites caused great trouble for many years.

Perhaps your parents own your house, or your father owns his store. Every day you pass many privately owned buildings. The idea that a person could own land was brought to America by the European colonists. The idea made no sense at all to the Indians. Indians thought that the land belonged to the whole tribe—not only the land on which the village stood

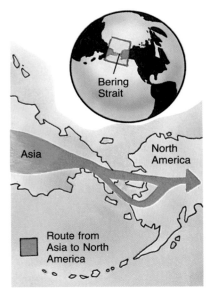

▲ *Thousands of years ago the Bering Strait between Asia and Alaska may have formed a "land bridge" that the ancestors of American Indians crossed to reach North America.*

▲ *An early painting of an American Indian woman and child. The child is holding an English doll.*

▲ *Indian tipis, made from buffalo hides, were easy to transport and quick to put up.*

Arizona has more Indians living on reservations than any other state has. The 160,000 Indians in the state come from 13 different tribes.

and the fields where crops grew, but also the woods, fields, and streams where the warriors hunted and fished.

Most Indians believed that every animal, plant, and natural object contained a spirit. They thought these spirits could be helpful when they were pleased, but they could also cause great harm when they were offended. Important spirits included those of the sun, fire, and water; the buffalo, eagle, and snake; and corn and tobacco. With all these spirits in the natural things surrounding them, it is not surprising that the Indians could not understand how any one person could "own" land. The Indians thought that they belonged to the land, not the other way around. This feeling was one that the white people did not understand.

In 1817, President James Monroe said that the Indians wanted too much land, and that they were getting in the way of "progress and just claims of civilized life." President Monroe was not the only white leader who was not interested in what the Indians needed. As the number of white settlers increased, more and more Indians were forced off their land. The first Indians to have trouble were those who lived close to the first white settlements in the East. And as white settlers moved westward, more

Indians were forced to fight for their land.

Another important difference between the white people and the Indians was that the settlers were organized. They had armies made up of persons from many towns to fight for the land they wanted. The Indians were separate groups of people. When one group was forced to fight for its land, the other groups did nothing to help. The Indians who agreed to move to new territory without fighting quickly discovered that they were no better off—all the white people's promises meant nothing. The Indian Wars of North America were bloody, terrible struggles that lasted nearly 300 years.

War, and the taking of the Indians' lands, were not the only kinds of trouble that white people gave to the Indians. White explorers and colonists also "gave" the Indians many diseases—measles, smallpox, tuberculosis. These diseases did not exist in the Americas until the whites came. Many thousands of Indians died of these diseases.

How the Indians Lived The way people live depends greatly on the area where they live. The Indians had to deal with problems of climate, altitude, soils—problems any civilization finds. Many stories about Indians tell of the cone-shaped *tipi*. Many Indians did live in tipis, but not all tipis were the same. The most familiar tipi was built by Plains Indians, such as the Blackfeet, the Cheyenne, and the Crow. This tipi had a carefully built frame of wooden poles, covered by buffalo hides that were sewn together. It was often 15 feet (4.5 m) across and 10 or 12 feet (3 or 3.6 m) high. This kind of tipi was cool in summer, warm in winter, and had an opening at the top so that smoke from an inside fire could escape. The opening could be closed when it rained. The Indians of the Plains moved often to stay near the buffalo herds. Their tipis could be put up or taken down in a few minutes.

Many Canadian Indians lived in tipis about half the size of the Plains tipi. The covering of the Canadian tipi was made of animal skins or tree bark. The skins were not sewn together, and tree branches were propped against the outside to hold the covering in place.

Not all Indians lived in tipis. The Indians who lived along the northwest coast of North America did not have to move very often. They needed sturdy houses to protect them from the weather. These tribes, including the Kwakiutl and the Tlingit, built houses of wooden planks. The largest of these houses were about 60 feet (18 m) long and were shared by several families.

Other tribes had other types of houses. The Iroquois *long house* was the most important type in the northeast. The long house was just that— about 18 feet (5.5 m) tall, 18 feet (5.5 m) wide, and 60 feet (18 m) long. Inside the long house were many rooms, each one serving as the "apartment" of one family. Many tribes built houses similar to the long house of the Iroquois, but smaller.

The Seminole Indians built *chickees*, houses that had no walls. The roof kept people dry. This was the only shelter needed in Florida's warm climate. Indians living on the western prairie built earth lodges, or wooden frames covered with mud and shaped much like an Eskimo igloo. Other dome-shaped houses, called *wigwams*, were built by the Indians of the Great Lakes area. The walls of a wigwam might be made of woven mats, bark, or animal hide. The Apache *wickiup* was also dome-shaped, with mat walls.

One group of Indians, the Pueblo, built apartmentlike houses of stone or clay. The largest of these buildings had five stories and held several hundred people. The buildings also served as forts—the ground floor had no doors or windows. The only entrance was by ladder to the roof. When the building was attacked, the ladders could be pulled up.

All of these houses had two things in common. First, they provided just the right amount of protection. The Indians of the far North needed thick walls to keep themselves from freezing. The Indians of warm southern areas needed cooling breezes. Each type of house was built of materials found where the Indians lived. Buffalo hides were easy to get on the Great Plains. Grass for woven mats was easy to get on the prairie. The northwest coast was covered with forests, so the people had no problem building wooden houses.

FOOD. The Indians spent much of their time finding food. Eastern Indians, such as the Iroquois and Lenni-Lenape, hunted, fished, and raised crops. The Indians in each region of North America had one basic type of food that was more important to them than any other type. Indians of the East and South depended on corn. Tribes of the Middle West gathered wild rice. Plains Indians once ate many kinds of foods. But when they obtained horses from the Spanish during the 1600's, they stopped farming and used all their time and energy to hunt buffalo. They ate the meat and used the skins to provide warmth. They also made

The Indian peace pipe was considered sacred. It was often smoked during religious, political, and social rituals. Most of all, it was used during the making of peace treaties.

▼ *A painting by the artist George Catlin of Plains Indians on a bear hunt. George Catlin produced many fine paintings of Indian life in the 1830's.*

◀ *A Cherokee chief in splendid ceremonial headdress.*

▲ *Most Indians today dress, work, and play like their fellow Americans. Traditional dress is still worn, however, for special holidays or ceremonial occasions.*

◀ *North American Indians, like Eskimos and South American Indians, belong to the Mongoloid race.*

▼ *Four Sioux Indian chiefs who once battled the white man: Sitting Bull (left), Swift Bear, Spotted Tail, and Red Cloud.*

ESKIMO
SUB-ARCTIC
NORTHWEST COAST
THE GREAT PLAINS
CALIFORNIAN
SEED PICKERS
SOUTHWESTERN DESERT
EASTERN WOODLANDS
ARAWAK
MEXICO-CENTRAL AMERICA

Eskimo
Eskimo
Kutchin
Aleut
Dog-rib
Yakutat
Tlingit
Haida
Tsimshian
Kwakiutl
Nootka
Chinook
Modoc
Klamath
Hupa
Yurok
Pomo
Flathead
Nez Percé
Blackfoot
Crow
Shoshone
Bannock
Wintun
Miwok
Chumash
Paiute
Mohave
Pima
Navaho
Yaki
Papago
Seri

Beaver
Sarsi
Yellow Knife
Chipewyan
Eskimo
Plains Cree
Assiniboin
Arikara
Hidatsa
Mandan
Cheyenne
Teton Sioux
Yankton Sioux
Arapaho
Ute
Cheyenne
Pawnee
Kiowa
Zuni
Hopi
Pueblo
Apache
Totonac
Aztec
Nahuatl

Eskimo
Wood Cree
Ojibwa
Santee Sioux
Ponca
Omaha
Iowa
Oto
Kansa
Osage
Caddo
Comanche
Tonkawa

Eskimo
Montagnais
Naskapi
Algonkin
Ottawa
Menominee
Winnebago
Sauk
Fox
Potawatomi
Miami
Kickapoo
Shawnee
Chickasaw
Choctaw
Natchez

Micmac
Abenaki
Penobscot
Huron
Mohican
Passamaquoddy
Wampanoag
Iroquois
Narragansett
Erie
Lenni-Lenape
Powhatan
Tuscarora
Cherokee
Catawba
Creek
Yamasee
Seminole

Lucayo
Arawak
Maya
Zapotec
Quiche
Mosquito

Ojibwa wigwam
Mandan earth lodge
Pomo reed & mat hut
Plains tipi
Navaho hogan
Apache wickiup
Caddo grass house
Pueblo
Natchez house
Creek Choko
Lenni-Lenape wigwam
Abenaki wigwam
Seminole chickee

A Bible for Indians was the first Bible to be printed in North America. In 1661, Rev. John Eliot had the Bible printed in the Algonkian language.

tools from the bones and found many different uses for other parts of the animals' bodies.

Indians who lived in what is now California gathered most of their food. They collected many kinds of seeds, fruits, and roots, but their most important food was acorns. The major food of the northwest Pacific Coast Indians was fish. Some hunted whales from 40-foot-long (12-m-long) dugout canoes. The Indians of Alaska and northern Canada depended on moose, caribou, and seals, as much as the Plains Indians depended on buffalo.

CLOTHING. Indian clothing, just like food and shelter, was closely related to how and where the Indians lived. The Plains Indians used buffalo hides to make robes, shirts, pants, dresses, and moccasins. Some tribes in warm areas wore light clothes made of woven bark. Others wore deerskin clothes. Before the arrival of Europeans, the Pueblo Indians of New Mexico and Arizona were the only people living in what is now the United States who wore clothing sewn from cotton cloth.

The work that the Indians did also depended, for the most part, on where they lived, and there were

strict rules about who should do what. In general, women did most of the day-to-day work, including farming and cooking. The men hunted, fished, and fought in times of war. On the Great Plains, it was the woman's job to take down the tipi and put it up again when a new campground was reached.

In nearly all tribes, men made most decisions. But women usually owned all the property, except horses and weapons. The Iroquois women's

▼ *Plains Indians were nomads, following the great herds of bison on which they depended. Their tipis were carried on wooden frames* (travois), *dragged by dogs or horses.*

council chose the chief, and women could declare war.

Indians of Central and South America The Indians of Central and South America had to get food, provide shelter, and make clothing, just as their North American brothers did. But two groups of Central American Indians—the Maya and Aztecs—and one group of South American Indians—the Incas—developed complicated societies that were much larger and better organized than any Indian group of North America.

The Maya civilization developed about A.D. 300 in the area that makes up present-day Honduras, Guatemala, and southern Mexico. The Maya were excellent astronomers and architects. Many of their buildings are still standing and are still admired today. At its height, the Maya Empire included more than one million people. The Maya were the only Indians of the New World to develop and use a form of writing.

Another large empire—the Aztec—grew up in Mexico during the 1200's. The capital city was Tenochtitlán, which stood where Mexico City is today. Experts say that Tenochtitlán had a population of 100,000 people when the Spaniards reached Mexico in the early 1500's. (London's populaton at the same time was less than 50,000 people!) The riches of the people and the size of the city amazed the Spaniards. The Aztecs developed a mighty army that helped them control a huge part of Central America for nearly 300 years. But the army was amazed (and frightened) by the guns and horses of the Spanish, and the Aztec Empire was quickly conquered by Spain.

Many Central American Indians of today are descendants of these two mighty civilizations. Many Mexican Indians still speak *Nahuatl*, the Aztec language. The Lacandone Indians, who live in Mexico's southern tip, are descendants of the Maya. The Lacandones' language, customs, and traditions all come from the ancient Maya civilization. The Lacandones have no empire, though. They live in

▲ *These Navaho women are weaving rugs on a hand loom. The Navaho reservation in Arizona and New Mexico is the largest in the United States.*

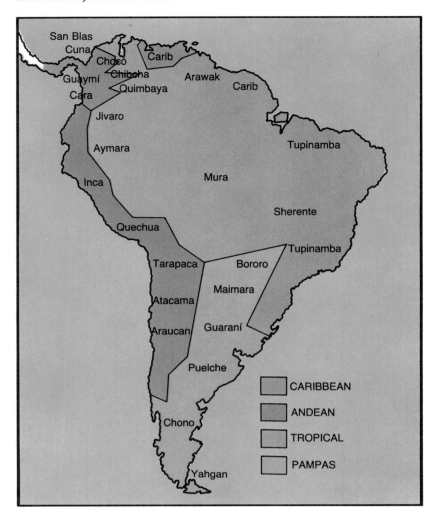

San Blas
Cuna
Choco
Guaymí
Chibcha
Cara
Quimbaya
Carib
Arawak
Carib
Jivaro
Aymara
Tupinamba
Inca
Mura
Sherente
Quechua
Tarapaca
Tupinamba
Bororo
Maimara
Atacama
Araucan
Guaraní
Puelche
Chono
Yahgan

CARIBBEAN
ANDEAN
TROPICAL
PAMPAS

diers and running messengers. The Inca civilization, as great as it was, never managed to develop wagons or any other kind of wheeled vehicles.

The ancestors of the Incas probably reached what is now Peru about 4,000 years ago. These Indians developed mining and metalworking beginning about A.D. 400. Like the Aztecs, the Incas had a great empire when the Spanish conquistadors arrived. And as they did with the Aztecs, the Spaniards quickly destroyed the Inca Empire.

Many other groups of Indians have lived or are living in Central and South America. The San Blas Indians live on tiny islands just off the mainland of Panama. They are good farmers and fishermen, and they build very good dugout canoes.

The fierce Jivaro Indians live in Ecuador and Peru. They have been known as cruel, bloodthirsty, head-hunting warriors since the 1500's. But they were peaceful when the Spaniards first arrived in their territory. Like many North American Indians, the Jivaro became warriors only when the Europeans refused to leave them

▼ *The features of this Mexican woman reveal her Indian origin, though three fourths of Mexicans are* mestizos—*of mixed white and Indian origin.*

thatched huts grouped in small villages in jungle clearings. They use primitive tools to farm the poor soil, and they hunt jungle animals.

Millions of Indians—most of whom live in the Andes Mountains of Bolivia, Ecuador, and Peru—speak *Quechua*, which was the language of the ancient Inca Empire. At its height, the Inca Empire stretched more than 2,500 miles (4,000 km) from north to south, and was larger in size than the ancient Roman Empire.

The ancient Romans were good engineers and builders, but the Incas were better. The roads they built and paved with stone over thousands of miles of mountains and deserts are still used by travelers. And Inca bridges still cross canyons thousands of feet deep. These great roads and bridges were built for the Inca sol-

alone. The Jivaro received their name from the thatched oval hut—*jivaria*—in which each family lives. The Jivaro have no tribal government, but they may follow one strong leader during a war.

In the southern part of South America, the land is poor and the climate is sometimes extremely cold. The Indians of this area have a constant struggle to stay alive. Each day they must find berries or nuts or catch fish. Ferdinand Magellan, the great explorer, and his men were the first whites to meet these Indians. The explorers saw the poor Indian huts covered with sea-lion skins and watched as the Indians shivered and threw more logs on their fires. Magellan named the region *Tierra del Fuego* (land of the fire). These Indians spent so much time and energy in their desperate hunt for food that they never developed any arts. They did not even have any baskets or pottery for their own use.

Indians Today The North American Indians who were forced onto reservations in the United States received little public attention for some time. They were not even recognized as U.S. citizens until 1924, when Congress passed a special law giving them citizenship and the right to vote. Government studies during the 1920's found that living conditions on many reservations were terrible. The national and state governments, as well as church groups, tried to improve conditions, but most attempts did little good. New programs, however, were begun by the U.S. government in the 1960's. These programs have been designed to help the Indians plan, develop, and manage businesses and build houses. Many of these programs are beginning to change the way Indians live. Also in the 1960's Indians became active in politics. This has helped them work for the rights the U.S. government promised them. Although the Indians

▲ *Peruvian Indians on the way back from market. They carry babies and bundles of goods on their backs.*

have managed to survive very terrible troubles, many problems still exist. Experts say that when Columbus reached the New World in 1492, there were about 850,000 Indians living in the territory that now makes up the United States. Wars and diseases brought about the death of huge numbers of Indians. In 1920, there were fewer than 250,000 Indians living in the United States. But since 1920, conditions have improved, and about 1,418,000 Indians live in the U.S. today.

For further information on:
Art History, *see* INDIAN ART, AMERICAN; TOTEM.
Famous Indians, *see* COCHISE; GERONIMO; JOSEPH, CHIEF; MAS-

When the white people first settled in America there were as many as 900 Indian languages. There were so many because the various tribes were widely separated over a huge area.

◀ *Bolivian Indians in a market in La Paz.*

▶ *The Jivaro, a South American Indian tribe, were once great warriors. A victorious Jivaro warrior would shrink the head of an enemy killed in battle.*

Toward the end of the Indian Wars, bands of Apache Indians fought against unbelievable odds. During 1881, fewer than 40 Apache braves fought and won battle after battle against U.S. troops, Texas Rangers, border guards, and ranchers in a campaign that went on for two months. In 1884, less than a dozen Apache warriors raided for a month across many miles of enemy territory. They spread terror and eluded 2,000 U.S. troops, while losing only one warrior.

SASOIT; OSCEOLA; POCAHONTAS; PONTIAC; POWHATAN; SEQUOYA; SITTING BULL; TECUMSEH.

History, *see* AMERICAN COLONIES; COLUMBUS, CHRISTOPHER; CONQUISTADOR; CUSTER, GEORGE; FRENCH AND INDIAN WAR; INDIAN WARS; LEWIS AND CLARK EXPEDITION; PIONEER LIFE; WESTWARD MOVEMENT; *article on each U.S. state.*

How Indian Tribes Developed, *see* AGRICULTURE, ANCIENT CIVILIZATIONS, BOW AND ARROW, CLIFF DWELLERS, FIVE NATIONS, HUMAN BEINGS, SHELTER.
For individual tribes see index at name.

INDIAN SUMMER see AUTUMN.

INDIAN WARS As colonists settled in the New World, they moved onto Indian hunting grounds. The Indians were forced to move or to fight for their lands. Most tribes refused to leave their lands just because the Europeans wanted them. So, many wars were fought, starting in the early 1600's. The last Indian War did not end until 1900. By then most Indians in the United States had been resettled on *reservations* (public land set aside for Indians).

Both colonists and Indians farmed and hunted. But the colonists thought that they could do whatever they wanted on the land. They did not know or care that each tribe thought its land was holy, and that each plant and animal contained a spirit that had to be respected.

The first major war between the colonists and Indians was fought in Virginia in 1622. By 1641, almost 35 years after the first colonists arrived at Jamestown, the powerful Powhatan Indians were destroyed. In 1637, New England colonists attacked a Pequot Indian town in Connecticut and killed all 600 people who lived there. Another New England war began in 1675. King Philip, whose Indian name was Metacomet, was chief of the Wampanoags and a brilliant soldier. He led attacks against several frontier towns in Massachusetts. But Metacomet was killed in 1676, and his people were sold as slaves.

As settlers crossed the Appalachian Mountains, they invaded more Indian territory, and the Indians fought to protect their hunting grounds. In 1763, Pontiac, a great chief of the Ottawas, led many tribes. Pontiac's warriors captured ten British forts and killed 2,000 settlers in Pennsylvania and Virginia.

The Delaware, Shawnee, and Cayuga tribes were defeated in Lord Dunmore's War in 1774. The war was fought because settlers wanted the lands of these Indians (now part of Ohio). More Ohio territory was captured from the Shawnee, Ottawa, Chippewa (Ojibwa), and Potawatomi Indians in the Battle of Fallen Timbers in 1794. Andrew Jackson fought the Creek Indians in 1814 and, as a result, acquired land in Georgia and Alabama.

The last Indian war to be fought east of the Mississippi River was the Seminole War, which lasted from 1835 until 1842. The Seminoles were forced to march from their Florida home to a reservation in Oklahoma. Thousands of Seminoles died on the terrible journey to the reservation. Some hid in the swamps of the Everglades, where their descendants still live today.

As Indian lands were taken over by settlers and the tribes were pushed westward, the Indians began to make treaties with the U.S. government. They promised to live peacefully on their reservations. They kept their promises. The government promised to allow the Indians to live and hunt on the reservation lands. But the government often broke its promises. Soldiers were sent to the reservations and the Indians were forced to move.

The Sioux and Cheyenne tribes fought many battles against the U.S. Army between 1854 and 1890. The Sioux were brave warriors who used horses in battle, which the eastern tribes had not done. General George A. Custer and the 250 soldiers he led were killed by the Sioux, led by the chiefs Crazy Horse and Sitting Bull, in the Battle of Little Big Horn, Montana, in 1876. In 1890, soldiers killed hundreds of unarmed Sioux prisoners, including women and children, at Wounded Knee Creek, South Dakota. The soldiers felt that they had now avenged Custer.

The Indians of the southern plains—the Cheyenne, Arapaho, Kiowa, and Comanche—also fought for their tribal lands. Battles took place over a period of more than 25 years, from 1865 to 1891. Many tribes from California, Oregon, and Washington also fought bitterly for their lands. The Nez Percé Indians lived in Idaho. They agreed to move to a reservation, but some settlers stole their horses and war broke out. The Nez Percé chief was named Joseph. His Indian name meant "thunder rolling in the mountains." Joseph led many successful raids on the white soldiers. When he saw that his people could never succeed in holding their lands, he led his whole tribe across 1,000 miles (1,600 km) of mountainous territory toward safety in Canada. When soldiers were finally able to surround the tribe, they were only 30 miles

(50 km) south of the Canadian border. They fought the soldiers for five days, before surrendering. They were then forced to move to a reservation.

The Navaho and Apache fought U.S. troops in many battles in New Mexico, Arizona, and Texas. The Apache managed to hold off the troops for 40 years, until 1900. The Apaches were brave warriors. Their best-known leaders were Cochise and Geronimo. The Apache defeat in 1900 was the end of the last Indian War.

ALSO READ: APACHE INDIANS; COMANCHE INDIANS; CUSTER, GEORGE; FRENCH AND INDIAN WAR; INDIANS, AMERICAN; IROQUOIS INDIANS; JOSEPH, CHIEF; NAVAHO INDIANS; NEZ PERCÉ INDIANS; PONTIAC; POWHATAN; SEMINOLE INDIANS; SIOUX INDIANS; SITTING BULL; WESTWARD MOVEMENT.

INDONESIA More than 13,500 islands lying southeast of the Asian mainland form the republic of Indonesia. They make up the world's largest island group and fifth most populous country. Java, Sumatra, Celebes, central and southern Borneo, and Irian Java are the principal areas. About three-fifths of the people live on the island of Java. (See the map with the article on ASIA.)

The high, mountainous islands of Indonesia have a humid, tropical climate. The rain and warmth make it a colorful country. Beautiful flowers,

▲ *Chief Red Eagle (William Weatherford) surrenders to General Andrew Jackson after the Battle of Horseshoe Bend in 1814. It was a decisive victory over the Creeks, who were forced to give up much of their land.*

In 1960, natural rubber accounted for about half of Indonesia's export trade. By 1980, this had fallen to one-fortieth of the total. In the same period, oil and natural gas exports rose from one-fourth to over three-fourths.

INDONESIA

Capital City: Jakarta (7,800,000 people).
Area: 782,663 square miles (2,026,940 sq. km).
Population: 188,000,000.
Government: Republic.
Natural Resources: Oil and natural gas, timber, copper, bauxite.
Export Products: Oil and gas, forest products, rubber, tin, coffee, fish.
Unit of Money: Rupiah.
Official Language: Bahasa Indonesian.

wild orchids, and ferns are plentiful. Monkeys, tigers, lizards called Komodo dragons, and a rare species of rhinoceros live in Indonesia.

Indonesian families usually live in small villages and grow crops for a living, including rice, sweet potatoes, corn, cassava, soybeans, and coconuts. Rubber, palm oil, sugarcane, tea, coffee, and tobacco are raised on plantations and are often exported. Forests produce ratan, teakwood, and kapok (used for life preservers and padding).

Indonesia has vast mineral resources that are largely untapped. Petroleum is Indonesia's most important mineral product. It is one of the world's largest suppliers of tin. Bauxite, coal, nickel, copper, iron ore, and manganese are also mined.

Indonesian dancing is famous throughout the world. Dancers from Bali are especially famous for their graceful temple dances.

The Indonesians speak over 250 languages. Their country's official language is Indonesian, the most widely spoken tongue. About 88 percent of the population are Muslims. But many people living on Bali are Hindus. About nine percent of the Indonesians are Christians.

Early explorers called Indonesia the Spice Islands. The first Dutch trading ships arrived in the late 1500's. For more than 300 years, the Dutch controlled the islands, known then as the Netherlands East Indies. The Japanese occupied the islands during World War II. Indonesians fought for and won their independence from the Dutch in 1949. Achmed Sukarno, the country's first president, established close ties with Communist China. General Suharto crushed a Communist plot to seize power in 1965 and was elected president in 1968, 1973, 1978, and 1983.

ALSO READ: ASIA, BORNEO, NEW GUINEA.

▼ *This bridge is typically Dutch, but it is in Jakarta, on the island of Java in Indonesia. The Dutch ruled these islands for several hundred years.*

INDUSTRIAL ARTS In junior and senior high school, students can learn about making and building things by taking courses in industrial arts. These courses teach the manual skills (the ability to work expertly with the hands) used in industry to make nearly all the products we use.

A course in *industrial drawing and design* teaches students how to design (plan) the appearance and structure of anything from an engine to a house. They learn how the object's parts fit together to make it work and what materials and tools are needed for its construction. They also learn how to read and to make detailed drawings, called *blueprints*, of the plan.

Students of *woodworking* learn how to design products, such as chairs or bookcases, that will best show the beauty of a piece of wood. They then learn how to join pieces of wood and other materials to make the creation strong and attractive. Students also learn different ways to finish wood, to give smoothness and shine to the product.

In *metalworking*, students learn how metals are made, including those that combine to make alloys. They also learn how to work with the tools used to bend metals into the desired shapes. Students often learn *welding* (joining pieces of metal together, usually with heat) and other machine-shop methods.

A course in *electricity and electronics* presents information on how electricity is *generated* (produced) and *transformed* (changed into power) for such things as heat and light. Students also learn how electronics is used for radio, TV, and radar. In this kind of class, students learn to make electric lights and bells themselves. They often learn to repair radios, stereos, and television sets.

A course in *auto mechanics* teaches students all the parts of an automobile engine and the way these parts work together. In this course, students learn to repair engines and to care for them properly. Some schools offer a course in *power mechanics*, in which students are shown how to use machines and engines that operate on electric power.

Graphic arts includes a study of all kinds of printing and photographic methods. Students learn to take and develop pictures and to set (arrange) the type used in printing written material as for a magazine.

Students who take courses in *plastics* and *ceramics* learn how to make things out of plastic, clay, concrete, stone, and glass. Students may make something as simple as a bowl or as complicated as a statue.

A knowledge of the industrial arts can save a consumer (buyer) money. In learning how to make an everyday product, a student learns how to tell good quality from poor quality. For example, someone who knows how to make a chair can tell whether a chair for sale in a store was made well and is worth its price.

Many communities provide vocational high schools where students take industrial arts courses to prepare them for jobs in industry immediately after graduation. For example, a boy or girl who has studied the graphic arts might get a job in a printing shop. Other students go on to technical schools to improve their skills or to learn new ones before getting a job. TV repair-workers, for example, usually have attended a technical school. Still other students go to college to prepare for a profession, such as architecture or engineering, that will require the knowledge and skills learned earlier in industrial arts.

▲ *Painting designs on china and pottery is a highly skilled job requiring a good deal of training.*

▲ *An industrial arts class is a wonderful opportunity for all those who want to develop manual skills.*

▲ *A power loom in Samuel Slater's cotton mill in Massachusetts in the early 1800's.*

Many people, however, study industrial arts to learn new hobbies. Someone with a knowledge of woodworking may refinish furniture for a hobby. A person with some experience in design and construction and a fondness for sailing might take up boat-building. Others make prints or ceramics in their spare time. A great many people like to take photographs. Knowledge of the industrial arts can make possible a hobby—or a career—that brings both pleasure and satisfaction.

ALSO READ: ARCHITECTURE, CAREER, DESIGN, GRAPHIC ARTS, MECHANICAL DRAWING.

INDUSTRIAL RELATIONS see LABOR UNIONS.

INDUSTRIAL REVOLUTION People have always manufactured weapons, tools, clothing, and other goods that they need. For many centuries, these things were made mostly by hand. They were manufactured in the home or by individual craftworkers. Most people also produced their own food on farms. About 200 years ago, this system began to change. People began to produce manufactured goods in large quantities in fac-

tories. They did not have time to tend their farms, and so they began to buy their food in stores. This geat change in the way people lived is called the Industrial Revolution.

England was the birthplace of this revolution. In that country, where *textiles* (cloth) were a major source of wealth, a new method of manufacturing was started, called the *domestic system*. Merchants would distribute large quantities of wool to be spun and woven by the people who wished to earn money by working in their homes. The merchants then paid the people for their work and sold the cloth at a profit.

In the mid-1700's, a Scotsman, James Watt, invented the first workable steam engine. This invention created a vast new source of power. A machine was invented that could spin several threads at one time. Then a mechanical loom was perfected for weaving the thread. The machines made large quantities of a product quickly and very cheaply. This process became known as *mass production*. The merchants who had grown rich from the domestic system began to buy the new machines. They built factories to house the machines, and employed workers to run them. By the mid-1800's, hundreds of factories had been built in England. Machines were also invented for making other products, such as pottery. The making of the machines themselves became a major industry.

It was not long before the Industrial Revolution began to spread from Britain to other countries. Despite attempts by the British government to prohibit the export of machinery and craftsmen, the textile industries of other European countries and the United States were soon being modernized. An American businessman, Francis Cabot Lowell, established one of the first modern textile factories in Waltham, Massachusetts. Soon the new industrial processes were well established.

▼ *At work in a coal mine in Britain in the early 1800's. Conditions in the mines were very bad, and men, women, and children worked for long hours there.*

Large amounts of iron were needed to make the new machines. Charcoal had always been used to *smelt* (melt) iron ore. But iron workers now discovered that iron ore could be smelted much more efficiently with coal. The mining industry grew with the need for coal and ore. A method soon was discovered for making steel from iron. Much stronger and more accurate machines could be made from this new metal. Manufactured goods and raw materials had to be transported to and from the factories. The shipping industry flourished. Railroads, canals, and new roads were built. The telegraph was invented, quickly speeding up the communications industry.

As the Industrial Revolution spread through Europe and the United States, people's lives began to change. The factories created many new jobs. But they also took some jobs away, by replacing people with machines. People came from far away to work in the factories, hoping to make more money than they could on the farms. They crowded into the new towns that were growing up around the factories. Living conditions were terrible in these towns. People had to work long hours, often in dangerous conditions. They were paid very little money. Many women and children were employed, even in the mines. Workers began to rebel against these injustices. They formed groups that were later called *labor unions*. They gathered to protest against their employers, and sometimes fights broke out, with violence on both sides. Eventually, laws were passed to correct many of the harsh

conditions, and the unions gained great strength.

The Industrial Revolution brought enormous wealth and power to England, parts of Europe, and the United States. But this wealth and power was mainly in the hands of the people who owned the industries.

Today, other nations throughout the world are going through their own industrial revolutions. The change from an agricultural to an industrial economy can now take place rather quickly. Modern industry has raised the standard of living in many countries, but it has also created many serious problems. Factory work is often dull and unrewarding, and workers need more responsibility. Too many people are still crowded into the cities. Waste products of factories have polluted the air and the water. But industry and governments everywhere are aware of these pollution problems and are using scientific methods to improve the kind of life people can have in a modern, industrial society. In recent years, a new kind of revolution has taken place in industry and commerce. The devel-

▲ *The New Lanark textile mills near Glasgow, Scotland, were built in the 1780's. They were later managed and part-owned by the philanthropist Robert Owen, who reduced working hours and provided housing for his workers.*

▼ *In the early 1800's steam was harnessed to pull trains. This picture of 1830 shows second-class carriages on the Liverpool-Manchester line in northwest England.*

The Industrial Revolution began in Britain, but after a time it spread to Europe and the United States. Between 1810 and 1812, an American named Frances Cabot Lowell visited textile mills in Lancashire, England. He returned to the United States and set up a textile factory in Waltham, Massachusetts. This factory was one of the first in the world to combine under one roof all the processes for making cotton cloth.

▼ *Chinese ink makers preparing and mixing the ingredients (soot, resin, oil, and gum). The Chinese began making ink around 1500 B.C.*

opment of the microchip has created a new revolution in technology that has become a kind of modern successor to the Industrial Revolution.

ALSO READ: AIR POLLUTION; CAPITALISM; CHILD LABOR; CITY; COAL; FULTON, ROBERT; IRON AND STEEL; LABOR UNION; MANUFACTURING; PETROLEUM; STOCKS AND BONDS; WATER POLLUTION; WATT, JAMES; WHITNEY, ELI.

INFECTION   see DISEASE.

INFLATION   see ECONOMICS.

INFRARED   see HEAT AND COLD.

INK   Whenever you read anything that is printed, such as a newspaper, book, or poster, you are reading something printed with ink. If you write with a pen, you are writing with ink. Ink is any liquid used for writing or printing. The first inks, thousands of years ago, were probably made from berry juice.

There are many kinds of ink, and most of them are made of coloring materials (dyes) dissolved in liquid. The kinds of dyes and liquids depend on what an ink is to be used for. For

example, the ink used in ballpoint pens is a thick, jellylike liquid. A ballpoint pen puts very little ink on paper, so the dye in the ink must have a very strong color. On the other hand, ballpoint ink would not work in a fountain pen. Fountain pen ink is more watery.

The liquid part of most printing inks dries very quickly. This quick drying is necessary because paper moves through modern printing presses very fast. Immediately after printing, the paper is stacked, cut, and folded. The ink would smear and run if it did not dry rapidly.

Invisible, or *sympathetic*, ink becomes invisible when it dries. Something must then be done to the dried ink to make it visible. It may be dipped in or sprayed with chemicals or it may be heated. Invisible ink used to be a favorite of spies, but the many modern ways of making invisible ink visible are so good that no invisible messages are really secret any more.

■ **LEARN BY DOING**

You can make invisible ink—just write your message with lemon juice. The writing will disappear as soon as it dries. But you can bring the message back by placing the paper on a warm heater or radiator for a few minutes. ■

ALSO READ: DYE, PRINTING.

INQUISITION   see SPANISH HISTORY.

INSECT   Insects make up about four-fifths of all the animals on Earth. More than 900,000 kinds of insects are known, and entomologists—scientists who study insects—discover about 7,000 new kinds of insects each year.

Insects' Survival   There are several reasons why insects are so plentiful.

First, they are able to live in more different environments than any other animals. Insects live on every part of the Earth, including the coldest polar regions, the hottest deserts, and the middle of the ocean. They live outdoors everywhere, and also in every kind of human dwelling place, from grass huts to brick apartment houses.

Second, most insects are small, needing little space and little food. About 21 acres (8.5 hectares) of the Earth's surface grow only enough food for one human being for a year, but the same space can feed more than a billion insects. One breadcrumb can provide a day's food for several ants. Most insects eat plants or other insects. Termites eat wood. Some insects, such as mosquitoes, live on the blood of human beings and other animals.

Third, insects reproduce very rapidly. For example, a single housefly lays 120 to 160 eggs. The eggs hatch in a few hours, and in 3 to 6 days these flies are full-grown, ready to produce another generation.

Harmful Insects Fortunately, only a few of the hundreds of thousands of kinds of insects are harmful to people. Perhaps the greatest harm is done by crop-eating insects, which destroy millions of tons of grains, vegetables, and fruits every year. Locusts and other grasshoppers destroy plants by eating the leaves. The larvae of many insects eat leaves and stems. Cutworms and corn borers, the larvae of two different moths, feed on many field crops. The larvae of Colorado beetles damage potatoes. Gypsy moth and tussock moth larvae can leave acres of trees without leaves.

A number of insects are household pests. Clothes moths damage wool clothes. Silverfish damage clothes, books, and leather. Weevils live in flour and other foods, and cockroaches invade all kinds of food.

Some insects carry serious diseases from one person to another, or from

animals to people. Certain mosquitoes carry malaria and yellow fever. Rat fleas carry bubonic plague. Lice carry typhus. Ordinary houseflies carry more than 40 serious diseases including typhoid, cholera, and dysentery.

Many insect pests can be controlled by using *insecticides*. (The suffix "-cide" means "killer of.") Insecticides that destroy crop-eating insects have helped to increase the world's food supply. Cattle and other farm animals can be washed or dusted with insecticides to protect them from harmful or annoying flies, ticks, mites, or lice. These farm animals grow larger and are healthier than unprotected animals. Insecticides can control deadly diseases, such as typhus and malaria, by spraying the breeding places of insects that spread these diseases.

The world today depends on insecticides to protect crops and animals and to help people avoid many serious diseases. But insecticides can cause many serious problems, and they must be used carefully and wisely. For example, DDT, which used to be widely used as a spray for crops, found its way into the water supply, affecting fish and other animals. Because of its harmful effects, the use of DDT was banned almost entirely by the U.S. government in 1972. Other insecticides kill useful insects at the same time as they kill pests.

▲ *Cicadas have wide heads with large compound eyes. They are related to leafhoppers, treehoppers, and scale insects. Cicadas make a chirping sound at night.*

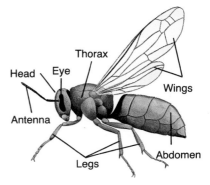

▲ *The parts of an insect showing the three very distinct sections of its body—head, thorax, and abdomen.*

▶ *Some insects are beautifully camouflaged in their natural surroundings. This lappet moth looks just like a dead leaf on the forest floor.*

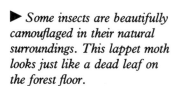

▲ *Horseflies have large, iridescent compound eyes, and beaklike, piercing mouthparts.*

It has been said that there are more species of insect still waiting to be discovered than the total number of different species of all other animals put together. It is also said that in the whole world there may be as many as 1,000,000,000,000,000,000 insects—over 300 million of them for each man, woman, and child alive.

Helpful Insects Many insects are helpful to people. Some are important pollen carriers. Bees, wasps, moths, and other insects that feed on nectar carry pollen from one flower to another, pollinating the flowers. The pollinated flowers eventually become fruits.

Some insects produce materials useful to people. Bees make honey and wax. Silkworms make silk.

Among the most helpful insects are those that prey on insect pests. Ladybird beetles eat great numbers of aphids, which are harmful to food and flower crops. Several kinds of wasps lay their eggs in caterpillars that eat food crops. The wasp larvae that hatch from the eggs eat the caterpillars. Certain flies, called tachinas, destroy squash bugs, mealy bugs, gypsy-moth larvae, and other harmful insects. Praying mantises eat grasshoppers, and dragonflies eat mosquitoes.

The Structure of Insects Although there are many different kinds of insects, all of them have bodies that set them apart from other kinds of animals. Every insect's body is divided into three main parts—a head, a thorax, and an abdomen. And every insect has three pairs of jointed legs. The head of an insect is, of course, at the front, the thorax is in the middle, and the abdomen is at the rear.

On an insect's head is a pair of antennae, which are for touch, taste, and smell. Every insect also has a pair of compound eyes, usually one on each side of the head. Each compound eye is made up of thousands of tiny lenses. Most adult insects also have three simple eyes that form a triangle on the forehead. The mouthparts of insects are either jaws used for chewing, or tubes used for piercing and sucking. A grasshopper has jaws, a housefly has a sucking tube, a horsefly has a rasping tongue and a sucking tube, and a mosquito has a tube for piercing and sucking.

An insect's six legs are attached to the thorax in three pairs. Each leg has five parts connected by joints. In some insects, the legs may look different and have different purposes. The front legs of a praying mantis are spiny and strong for grasping prey. The rear legs of a grasshopper are very long and strong for jumping.

Many insects have two pairs of wings, which are attached to the thorax. In some insects, such as beetles and grasshoppers, the front pair is thick and tough, and serves as a cover that protects the other pair. A beetle's heavy front wings protect most of its body, too. An insect's wings may be transparent, as in dragonflies, or covered with brightly colored scales, as in

▲ *The Goliath beetle is the largest of all insects. An adult goliath beetle can measure up to 4 inches (10 cm) long.*

▼ *The familiar honeybee is important to the plant world as a pollinator.*

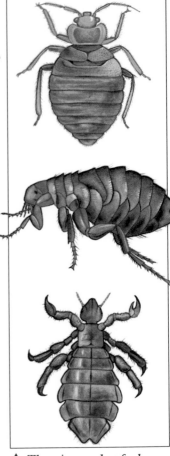

▲ *This walking stick insect is wingless. Many tropical stick insects have wings.*

▲ *Three insects that feed on people. The bedbug (top) hides by day and sucks blood at night. The human flea (center) can jump many times its own height to reach its prey. It also sucks blood, as does the human louse (bottom).*

▼ *Silverfish are primitive, wingless insects that can cause damage to books and clothing.*

▶ *The black armored head of this termite soldier has a snout that squirts a poisonous liquid to deter enemies.*

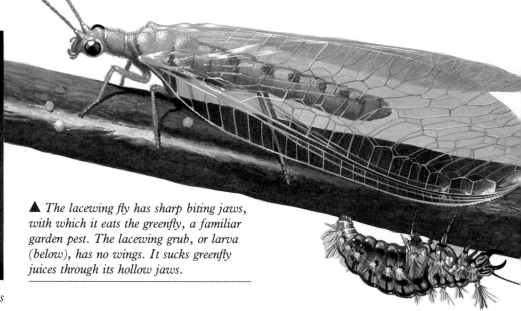

▲ *A bee-killer wasp carries its victim securely under its body on the way to its burrow.*

▲ *The lacewing fly has sharp biting jaws, with which it eats the greenfly, a familiar garden pest. The lacewing grub, or larva (below), has no wings. It sucks greenfly juices through its hollow jaws.*

The flea is the champion jumper of the animal world. It can jump 100 times its own height and do a broad jump 200 times its own length. This is like a human being jumping over 500 feet (150 m) into the air and achieving a long jump of over 1,000 feet (300 m).

moths and butterflies. Some insects' wings carry them long distances. Others are used only for short, quick flights from danger. Some kinds of insects, such as fleas, have no wings.

An insect's abdomen is made up of ten sections, or segments. The abdomen contains some of the organs for digesting food, as well as the organs of reproduction.

The outer part of an insect's body is made up of a tough material called *chitin*. This is the insect's skeleton. It covers and protects the insect's inner organs.

In an insect's head, there is a knot of nerve tissues serving as a kind of brain. From this brain, pairs of nerves run the length of the body, connecting smaller knots of nerves called *ganglia*. From ganglia, nerves go to, and return from, the organs.

Along both sides of an insect's body are rows of openings, called *spiracles*, through which an insect breathes. Air entering a spiracle goes through a tube called a *trachea*. This tube divides into smaller and smaller branches that carry air to inner parts of the insect's body. In insects, blood does not carry oxygen. However, insect blood does carry food substances and special chemicals (hormones) that control growth.

Many kinds of insects have devel-

oped special organs. Insects that make sounds—grasshoppers (including katydids) and crickets—have organs of hearing. These are located either on the front legs or in the first segment of the abdomen. Some moths, too, have organs of hearing. Insects have short hairs that are organs of touch, especially around the mouth. Other insects have special glands that produce poisons. And some insects have special organs, such as stingers, to defend themselves or attack others.

Reproduction and Growth A female insect has organs called *ovaries* that form and store eggs. At the rear of the abdomen is a tube called an *ovipositor*, through which the female lays the eggs. Some insects, such as queen termites, lay hundreds of thousands of eggs. A male insect has *testes*, organs that produce *sperm*, male sex cells. It also has an organ to deposit the sperm into the female's body.

All insects hatch from eggs. Some look much like adults when they hatch. Newly hatched grasshoppers look like "grown-ups," except they have no wings or sex organs. these young insects are called *nymphs*. Periodically the nymph sheds its skeleton, grows larger, and forms a new, larger skeleton. This process, which is controlled by hormones produced by the nymph, is called *molting*. A nymph usually goes through four to six molts before becoming an adult, but there may be more. The process of a young insect gradually changing into an adult is called *incomplete metamorphosis*. Each successive stage is more like the adult insect.

Many kinds of insects go through major changes in body form on their way to becoming adults. In this process, a wormlike creature called a *larva* hatches from the egg. Grubs, maggots, and caterpillars are three kinds of larvae. The larva feeds and grows for a period lasting from a day or two to many months. When fully grown, the larva produces a liquid that hardens when it comes into contact with air. The larva completely covers itself with the liquid. The hardened covering is called a *pupa case*, and the insect inside is a *pupa*.

The pupa undergoes great changes and finally breaks out of the pupa case as a fully developed insect, called an *imago*. This process of growth in four main steps—egg, larva, pupa, and imago—is called *complete metamorphosis*. Moths, butterflies, mosquitoes, and flies are some insects that go through complete metamorphosis.

ALSO READ: ANIMAL, ANIMAL KINGDOM, ANT, BEE, BUTTERFLIES AND MOTHS, DRAGONFLY, DROSOPHILA, FLY, GLAND, HORMONE, LOUSE, METAMORPHOSIS, MOSQUITO, PARASITE, WASPS AND HORNETS.

INSECT-EATING PLANT Insects destroy many, many plants each year. You have probably seen many trees, flowers, bushes, and vegetables spoiled by insects. But what is surprising is that some plants "fight back" by eating insects. The plants trap the insects and then digest them. Insects are not the only food of these plants. Like other green plants, their leaves produce starch, which the

▲ *The sundew traps insects with a sticky fluid at the tips of little spines on its leaves. The insect juices make up for the lack of food in poor soil.*

plants use as food. Insect-eating plants live in wet places, where the soil lacks nitrogen, which is important to plant growth. These plants get nitrogen from the insects' bodies.

The largest insect-eating plant is the *pitcher plant*. The leaves of this plant form a pitcher-shaped container that holds rainwater. The rim of the pitcher has scales or stiff hairs pointing downward. Insects that enter the "pitcher" are unable to climb out because of the hairs or scales. In their struggle, the insects fall into the water and drown. They are digested by the plant.

The *sundew* has leaves covered with sticky tentacles. When an insect lands on the leaf the tentacles bend towards the insect, trapping it, and secrete an acid that digests it.

The *Venus's-flytrap* has leaves folded in the middle, so that each leaf looks like a clamshell. Around the edges of each leaf are toothlike spikes, and on the surface of each half of the leaf are sensitive bristles. When an insect touches one of these bristles, the halves close suddenly, like a mouth snapping shut. The spikes form a cage that traps the insect. Venus's-flytraps catch mostly crawling insects, because most flying insects are quick enough in taking flight to escape.

The *bladderwort* is a water plant that has many one-eighth-inch-long (3-mm-long) bladders, each with a trapdoor equipped with sensitive bris-

▲ *The pitcher plant of North America is so-called because of the shape of its leaves. The leaves hold rainwater, and when insects fall in, they drown.*

Water surface

Sac, showing trapdoor

▲ *The bladderwort traps water fleas in small sacs that grow underwater on the plant's finely divided leaves.*

tles. When an insect touches a bristle, the trapdoor swings inward with a rush of water that sweeps the insect into the bladder.

ALSO READ: FLOWER, PLANT.

INSULATION A ski jacket keeps you warm in winter. It "insulates" your body and prevents heat from escaping into the cold air. Mammals that live in cold climates grow thick coats to protect them from cold weather. Woolen and fur clothing insulates people from the cold. The air trapped in fur or wool provides excellent insulation. The word "insulation" comes from the Latin word *insula*, which means "island." Insulation surrounds an object and prevents the passage of not only heat, but also electricity and sound.

Asbestos, cotton, wool, rubber, and wood are good *insulators*. Glass and porcelain also insulate. Metals are very poor insulators but are very good *conductors* (substances that carry heat, electricity, or sound).

A house must be insulated to keep the heat in during cold weather and out during hot weather. Thick stone or brick walls are good for this purpose. Wooden frame houses must have both outside walls and inside walls. The air space between these walls provides some insulation, but it is better to fill this space with an insulating material such as rock wool, or fiberglass. The roof of a house must be well insulated to keep hot air, which rises, from escaping from the top of the house in cold weather. Roof insulation also keeps the summer sun from piling up heat in the house.

Metal wires, which are good conductors, are used to carry electricity. To keep people from getting a severe shock, the wires are insulated with a covering of rubber, plastic, or tightly woven cotton fabric.

A home or apartment is insulated for sound in much the same way it is heat insulated. Single walls must be thick enough, or double walls must have enough space between them, to keep sound out. Many people who live in thin-walled apartments can hear sounds from the next apartment. Sound insulation is also used in many places to keep sounds from becoming too loud and too confusing. Theaters, concert halls, restaurants, and other large rooms have special coverings on their walls and ceilings. These coverings, such as fiberboard, absorb much of the sound in a room, whereas sound bounces off hard stone and plaster walls. Curtains and draperies are also effective in absorbing sound and reducing noise level.

■ **LEARN BY DOING**

You can see how insulation works by performing an experiment. You will need a very large cardboard carton and two smaller boxes, such as salt or cereal boxes, with the tops removed. You will also need a small table lamp with a 40- or 60-watt bulb, two thermometers, and some shredded newspaper.

Stuff one of the smaller boxes with the newspaper, placing one thermo-

▼ *Feathers are good insulators. Mountain climbers rely on feather-filled clothes and sleeping bags to keep them warm in temperatures well below freezing. The feathers trap a layer of air, warmed by the body, between the skin and the cold air outside.*

meter in its center. Place the other thermometer into the other small box, which has no newspaper stuffing. Now put both small boxes into the carton with the lighted lamp between them.

Allow the thermometers to be exposed to the heat of the lamp for half an hour. Then check them. What has happened? If you extend the time to one hour, what will happen? Can you explain this method of insulation? ■

ALSO READ: ELECTRICITY, HEAT AND COLD, SOUND.

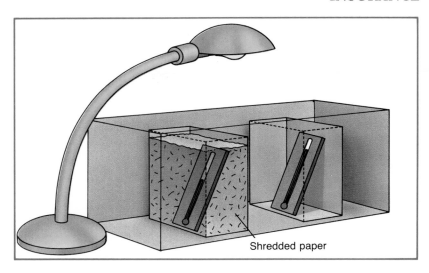
Shredded paper

INSURANCE An accident can cause severe injury to people and costly damage to property. Safety measures are the best protection against accidents. But when accidents do happen, having insurance can protect you.

Insurance is a kind of protection sold by insurance companies. It is based on the fact that a lot of people share the risks (and costs) of losses. For example, a person wishing to buy automobile insurance will pay a certain amount of money, or *premium*, to an insurance company. In return the insurance company will issue a *policy*, or contract, to the individual. The company agrees to pay for all or part of the losses or damages to, or caused by, that person's car. At the same time, thousands of other people are also paying the company for the same kind of insurance. Most of these people will never have an accident, so the insurance company will never have to pay them money for any damages or losses. But the money that these thousands of people have paid to the company is more than enough to cover the losses or damages that some of them will have.

What do insurance companies do with the extra money? Some of the money is kept for a constant supply of cash. Some of the money is used for operating expenses—salaries, rent, supplies. And some is invested for profit.

The *premium rate*, or cost of insurance, is based upon averages. This means that the company will figure out how many times something happens, or is likely to happen, during a given time in a certain place. Then the company decides what chance the policy holder has of being involved in such an event. For example, an automobile owner living in a big city will be more likely to have an accident than one who lives in a small town where traffic is lighter. So the automobile insurance usually costs more in and around big cities.

People can buy many other kinds of insurance. Many musicians are insured in case anything happens to injure their hands. People who plan to vacation in a sunny place can be insured against rain that could spoil their vacation. Someone who supports a family can buy life insurance so that when he or she dies, the company will pay money to the family. Fire insurance is bought so that if a house or apartment is damaged or destroyed by fire, the owner will have enough money to replace any losses. A homeowner's insurance policy may also include protection of such valuable items as cameras, stereos, jewelry, and silver. Health insurance helps to pay doctors' and hospital bills. Many farmers also buy insurance against crop losses caused by nature, such as earthquakes and floods.

It is estimated that the average household in the United States pays more than $1,500 a year in insurance premiums.

Many people buy life, health, homeowners, and automobile insurance. When a person who has bought life insurance dies, the insurance company pays money to his or her family. Health insurance helps to pay for medical bills. If a home is damaged by fire, or if items in the home are stolen, homeowners insurance will cover most losses. Liability insurance is often included in automobile policies. This means that if a driver has an accident in which a person is injured, the driver's insurance covers the medical bills of the injured person. If a driver is sued, liability insurance is used to pay the lawsuit.

Perhaps the most famous insurers in the world are Lloyds of London. This company is reputed to insure anything, from racehorses to supertankers and space rockets.

Hartford, Connecticut is known as the insurance capital of the world with some 50 insurance companies having their headquarters there. More insurance business is carried out here than anywhere else in the world.

ALSO READ: CHANCE AND PROBABILITY, STATISTICS.

INTEGRATION see CIVIL RIGHTS MOVEMENT, BLACK AMERICANS.

INTELLIGENCE Scientists define intelligence as the ability to learn or to understand. People who are intelligent learn what they are taught easily and quickly. Intelligent persons also remember what they have learned. This knowledge can then be used in new situations or problems. Intelligent persons faced with some problem or situation that they have never met before will use their knowledge and memory of situations in the past to solve the problem.

Many psychologists believe that intelligence can be measured with various kinds of tests. These scientists believe that if a person can deal intelligently with some problem in a test, he or she will also deal intelligently with problems in everyday life.

Psychologists express the results of an intelligence test in a number called an IQ (*intelligence quotient*). To determine this number, they first give tests to find the person's mental age. Two young people of 8 and 16 may both have a mental age of 12. The younger person has obviously developed faster than the older. But their mental age does not show the difference in their rates of mental growth. The mental age of the younger person is far above his or her chronological age (age in years). But the older person's mental age is far below his or her chronological age. Therefore, psychologists developed the formula

$$IQ = \frac{MA \text{ (mental age)}}{CA \text{ (chronological age)}} \times 100.$$

This means that the person's mental age is divided by his or her chronological age. The quotient is multiplied by 100, and the number that results is

Of all the nations that have produced figures for their national IQ, Japan comes first with a figure of 111. It is believed that more than a tenth of the Japanese people have IQs greater than 125.

▶ *A young chimpanzee watches its mother fish for termites. The young chimp will soon learn to feed in the same way. Intelligent animals learn by copying their parents.*

the IQ. This number represents the way that someone's intelligence compares with that of other people of his or her age. The 8-year-old person's IQ is 150; the 16-year-old's is 75.

But many people believe that intelligence tests do not really measure someone's ability. Many tests seem to measure *what* someone has learned rather than how quickly or slowly he or she can learn. Other people think that intelligence cannot be measured accurately.

What makes one person intelligent and another not so intelligent? Are people born with the basic intelligence that they will have all their lives? Is intelligence affected by a person's home life or the number of books he or she reads? Scientists are still studying these questions.

Human beings are the most intelligent animals. People have built cities, written books, and traveled to the moon. Since a human being is certainly not the biggest animal, or the animal with the biggest brain, intelligence cannot be measured by size. But studies of other animals are showing that a human being is definitely not the *only* animal with intelligence.

Other animals can communicate with each other, but they cannot read. They cannot do mathematics or build complicated things like automobiles or airplanes. Still, animals learn very quickly the things they have to know in order to stay alive and healthy. Animals also remember things they have learned.

An animal in the jungle knows who its enemies are, and it keeps out of their way. It knows what foods are good for it and how to find these foods. Animals teach these things to their young.

Many people believe that animals are not intelligent at all. These people say that animals have "instincts," not "intelligence." An "instinctive" act is something done automatically without having to learn it. For example, a newborn baby knows automatically how to suck milk from its mother's breast. No one has to teach the baby how to suck milk. Sucking is an instinct.

Monkeys in the jungle live together in large groups. Sometimes there are hundreds of monkeys living together. Yet, each baby monkey knows its own mother. The mothers can always tell their own babies from the other babies.

Some animals can act in very intelligent ways. Dolphins even have a language. They can "talk" to each other by making whistling and clicking sounds. If a dolphin is in danger, it can call other dolphins to help it. Dolphins can even work together and get a complicated job done that one dolphin alone could not do. They often work together without seeing each other. They talk to each other in their language over long distances and coordinate a "plan."

Many animals can be trained to do things that they do not otherwise do. Dogs can be trained to do tricks and to perform useful tasks such as leading blind people or herding sheep. Lions, tigers, seals, bears, and chimpanzees may be trained to perform in circuses. Rats use intelligence to get at food that seems out of their reach. They also learn to avoid food that has been poisoned.

ALSO READ: LEARNING, MEMORY, REASONING.

INTEREST If a person borrows money, he expects to pay for the use of it. The amount he pays is called interest. In the same way, a company may sell stocks or bonds to investors to raise money, and pay interest on the shares to compensate the investors.

The amount of interest is calculated as a percentage—that is, so many dollars for every hundred dollars loaned or invested. If a borrower is paying 8 percent, he pays $8 every year for the use of every $100 borrowed.

Simple interest is just a straight annual payment. *Compound interest* is the result of adding the interest to the

▲ *Robots are not intelligent. They cannot learn and have to be programmed by humans. This robot, called ROMAN, is used in the nuclear industry.*

The highest tested IQ was achieved by Marilyn Mach vos Savant of St. Louis, Missouri. As a child of 10 she scored a record IQ of 230.

▲ *A room in Syon House, near London, England, designed by Robert Adam. In the 1700's, Adam created grand interiors in the classical style of ancient Greece and Rome.*

▼ *A traditional Japanese interior is characterized by low furniture, matting on the floor, and cushions in place of chairs. The design is simple and harmonious.*

sum borrowed. In the above example at the end of the first year the $8 would be added to the $100 borrowed, so the second year's interest would be paid on $108, and would be $8.64.

ALSO READ: STOCKS AND BONDS.

INTERIOR DECORATING Interior decorating is the art of making rooms attractive, comfortable, and useful. It involves not only selecting decorations but also planning the design of rooms and other interior areas.

People who earn a living doing this are called *interior designers* or *interior decorators*. They are trained in the use of space, color, light, fabrics, and furniture. Most people, however, do their own interior decorating. They learn about decorating by looking at different styles of furniture and other items in stores and in other people's homes. Decorating magazines and catalogs also give many good ideas.

History No one knows when people first thought of making their homes beautiful. In ancient Egypt, Greece, and Rome, the upper classes had colorfully decorated homes. The walls and ceilings were often painted with scenes or brightly colored designs. Soft cushions and various textiles were used to cover long sofas and wooden chairs. The ancient Romans carefully planned their rooms according to how these rooms were used. They used great artistic skill in making furniture and room decorations.

After the Roman Empire fell, interior decoration became unimportant in Europe. Furniture was simple—usually just stools, tables, and storage boxes. Europeans traveling to the Middle East during the Crusades discovered the beautiful decorations and carved furniture of the Orient. Trade routes with the Middle East were set up. By the 1400's, wealthy Europeans were buying Oriental furniture and copying Oriental designs. Ruling families became *patrons* of decorators. They supported the decorators in exchange for having rooms beautifully furnished. Walls were hung with velvet draperies, mirrors, tapestries, and handmade wallpaper. Some furniture was *gilded* (covered with gold). Fine woods were used for chairs, tables, beds, and chests. Some pieces of furniture were beautifully carved.

During the 1600's and 1700's the wealthy people of France introduced decorated plaster ceilings, delicate fabrics, and huge glass chandeliers that held many candles. The French used fancy woods and materials like brass and tortoiseshell for furniture, which was light and graceful. As trade with the Orient expanded, styles of decoration from China and Japan became popular.

There were American styles of furnishing too, based on those of Europe. The earliest is now called Early American and is still popular, as is the Federal style of the early 1800's.

After the Industrial Revolution, a lot of furniture could be factory-made at lower prices. Many people, not just the wealthy, could then afford at least some beauty at home.

Techniques of Decorating Planning is an important part of interior decoration. The designer or decorator

must first list the activities that take place in each room. Will the living room be used to entertain friends? Will people read and relax there? Will people gather together in the living room at night to watch television? The answers to these and other questions will help the designer decide how to arrange the room. If the room is used for entertaining friends, comfortable chairs should be arranged so that people can talk together easily. If the room is used for reading, it will need good lighting. If people will be watching television in the living room, the television must be placed so that everyone will be able to see it.

The designer must also study the shape of the room. How long is it and how wide? How many windows and doors does it have? What is the easiest way for people to pass through the room? (This is called the *traffic pattern*.) These things decide where furniture goes.

The designer must think about the floor, too. Is it made of hard polished wood or linoleum tiles? Wood floors are attractive, but walking on them can be noisy. If the room is in an apartment with people living below, rugs or carpeting will probably be needed to lessen the noise.

When the designer or decorator has studied the room and how it is used, he or she then decides what colors would be best in it. The choice of color is important because colors are connected with moods or feelings. Reds and oranges usually have a warm feeling, while blues and bluegreens have a cool feeling. Bright colors often put people in a happy mood, while dark, dull colors put them in a sad mood. Also, light colors make rooms seem larger, and dark colors make them seem smaller. The designer must consider all these things when choosing a *color scheme*.

Color schemes can be a set of blending colors or contrasting colors. *Blending colors* are those that are similar, such as yellow and orange.

Contrasting colors are those that are quite different from each other, such as red and green. Different shades of the same color can also be used. A designer usually uses some light and some dark colors in every room.

A designer or decorator picks furniture that fits the activities and tastes of the people who use the room. Many people like modern, *contemporary* furniture, which has plain, undecorated lines and can be made of wood, metal, fabric, or plastics. Other people feel more comfortable with traditional furniture modeled after furniture styles of the past. Traditional furniture is usually made of wood and fabrics only. Designers will often combine different styles of furniture in one room.

Accessories are the ornaments used in a room to give it "personality." They include lamps, cushions, vases, pieces of pottery, and pictures. Accessories also include things such as plants, a display of a collection, or other special objects. Such accessories in a room tell something about the people who live there.

ALSO READ: ANTIQUE, CARPETS AND RUGS, COLOR, FURNITURE, HOUSE, LIGHTING.

▲ *This modern bathroom is designed to be both functional and attractive at the same time. Modern materials used in bathrooms and kitchens are durable and easy to clean.*

Until the 1500's rich people decorated the walls of their rooms with tapestry, velvets, and damasks. Then it was discovered that a much cheaper and quite pleasing effect could be had by covering the walls with sheets of paper made for the linings of books. The designs were probably checkered or marbled and the sheets were only about 12 by 16 inches (30 by 40 cm). They were nailed to the walls.

The United States has four time zones: Eastern, Central, Mountain, and Pacific. These zones are 5, 6, 7, and 8 hours respectively behind Greenwich Mean Time.

▼ *The world's time zones. There is one hour's time difference for every 15 degrees of longitude. The date changes at the International Date Line, which follows approximately the 180-degree meridian.*

INTERNATIONAL DATE LINE

If you look at a map of the world, or a globe, you will see lines that extend north and south between the poles. These are the lines of *longitude*. They are also called *meridians*. The globe is divided into 360 parts, or *degrees*. Each degree of longitude represents 1/360 of the distance around the globe. These imaginary lines make it possible to tell the location of a place east or west from the *prime meridian*. The prime meridian, which runs through Greenwich, England, is regarded as zero degrees. Every place in the world is located a certain number of degrees east or west of the prime meridian. Pittsburgh, Pennsylvania, for example, is 80 degrees west of the prime meridian.

Starting from any place on Earth and moving in a straight line east or west, you must cross 360 degrees of longitude to get back to where you started. As the Earth rotates, the path of the sun seems to move from east to west. This means that the sun seems to move 15 degrees west every hour. When it is noon in England, it is five hours before noon (7 A.M.) on the east coast of the United States. When it is noon on the east coast of the United States, it is three hours before noon (9 A.M.) on the west coast.

But where does the date change? The nations of the world have agreed that the date changes at 180 degrees longitude, the 180th meridian. This imaginary line is called the International Date Line. It runs from pole to pole, mostly through the Pacific Ocean. The Date Line does not follow the 180th meridian exactly. It bends to the east to include Siberia with Russia. Then it bends to the west to include the Aleutian Islands with Alaska. It bends to the east to keep all the Fiji Islands together.

Each date begins on the west side of the Date Line and ends on the east side. If you could stand just east of the line and your friends could stand just west of it, they would be one whole day (24 hours) ahead of you. You could watch them open their presents and eat Christmas dinner—but for you, it would still be Christmas Eve. And as they watched you open your presents and eat Christmas

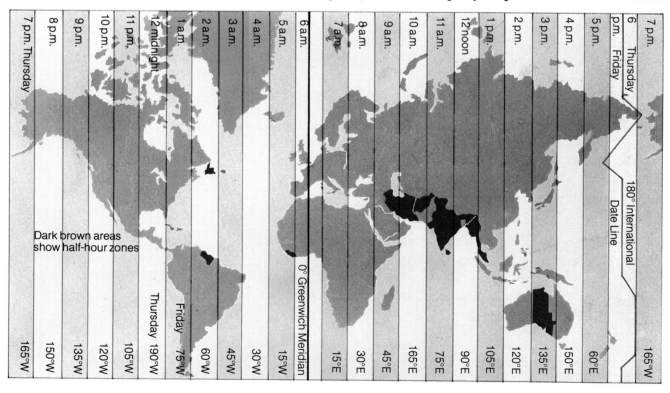

Dark brown areas show half-hour zones

dinner, their calendar would tell them it was December 26!

ALSO READ: LATITUDE AND LONGITUDE, MAP, TIME.

INTERNATIONAL LAW Nations, like people, are guided by certain customs and rules. The rules that guide the way nations behave are known as international law.

The idea of international law was developed in the 1600's by the Dutch statesman, Hugo Grotius. Grotius described certain rules that he thought all nations should obey. These rules would be based on custom—the way nations usually act. They would also be based on treaties—written agreements signed by two or more nations. In the 1800's and early 1900's, the major Western nations of the world met together and agreed upon a system of international law. For example, these laws state that in peacetime every nation has a right to govern its own territory and to control its ambassadors and embassies abroad. A nation must declare war before attacking another nation. Soldiers wounded in war must be given medical care. Warring armies must not pass through the land of a *neutral* nation, or one that favors neither side in war.

If nations do not obey international laws today, they may be urged to do so by an international organization, the United Nations. *Sanctions* (penalties for disobedience) may be applied against the offending country. For example, other countries may be forbidden to trade with that country. The International Court of Justice, which was set up by the United Nations, also helps to settle international disputes by the rules of international law.

ALSO READ: INTERNATIONAL RELATIONS, LEAGUE OF NATIONS, TREATY, UNITED NATIONS, WAR.

INTERNATIONAL RELATIONS
Relations among nations are somewhat like those among members of a family. Most family members want to get along with each other. Most nations want to get along with other nations. Family members want to feel secure in their home. Nations want to feel secure. No nation wants to live in fear of attack by another country. Each nation wants to govern itself as it wishes, without interference from other nations.

The guiding factor in family relationships is usually love. Members of a family are concerned about and help one another because they love each other. The guiding factor in international relations is usually *self-interest.* Nations help each other if doing so will benefit themselves in some way. Each nation looks out for itself and is mainly interested in its own welfare.

How Does Self-interest Work? A nation may protect its own interests in several ways. The most obvious way is to build a large, well-trained army, with modern weapons. Even if the army never goes into battle, its very existence keeps other nations from interfering in that country's affairs or invading its land. Some nations have gained a great deal for themselves through international trade. If a country has a much-needed product, such as oil, or if its industry is very strong, it can make agreements to supply other nations with products that they need. This increases a country's income. The strong trading nation can

▲ *A meeting of the General Assembly of the United Nations. This international peacekeeping body was set up in 1945. Today, it has more than 150 members.*

▼ *A Norwegian soldier, part of a U.N. peacekeeping force in Lebanon. Forces such as these act like policemen, trying to stop fighting in troubled areas.*

▲ *The signing of the Rhodesia ceasefire agreement in 1979. The country's white rulers had refused to agree to majority rule by black Africans. In this case, intense international pressure, plus a guerilla war inside the country, finally led to independence under a majority government.*

In the United States the President is responsible for foreign policy. He is advised by the Secretary of State and the Department of State, as well as by the National Security Council.

stop supplying needed products (or threaten to stop supplying them) in order to get what it wants from other nations. A nation that buys a great deal from one country can threaten to start buying from some other country if the nation from whom it buys begins to interfere.

Probably the best place to see national self-interest at work is in international negotiations. Nations come together to discuss their differences and try to reach an agreement that is acceptable to all of them. In the early stages of negotiations, each nation usually states its position. It tells the other what it wants. As negotiations progress, each nation sees that it cannot have everything it wants. Each must decide what *concessions* it will make. Each nation must *concede* (give up) some things it wants in order to come to agreement on other things. Each nation tries to concede only the less important things. A nation will not concede anything that is important to it. Each nation looks out for its own self-interest—trying to get as much out of the negotiations as possible, while conceding as little as possible.

Economics Every nation wants wealth, because wealth creates a better standard of living for its citizens. It also brings power. The search for wealth often brings nations into con-

tact with one another. In earlier times, this search led some nations to establish colonies in other lands. These colonies provided raw materials for the industries of the colonizing nation and markets for its goods. Throughout history, countries have increased their wealth by trading with one another. Today, nations in the same geographic area have formed associations to increase their economic or political power. One of these is the European Economic Community, or Common Market.

History International relations have been conducted in many ways. In ancient times, strong nations such as Rome conquered territories and built great empires. During the Middle Ages and Renaissance, most of western Europe was made up of small territories ruled by princes. These rulers were continually struggling for power among themselves. European nations, as we know them, began to be formed in the 1300's. They were based on the idea of *national sovereignty*. This meant that each nation was independent and had the right to govern itself.

Nations tried to keep peace by preventing any one nation from getting so much power that it was a threat to the other nations. This system is called a *balance of power*. When one nation showed signs of becoming too powerful, other nations would form an *alliance* against it. The allied nations agreed to help one another in case of political interference, military attack, or even for economic reasons. An alliance on one side often led to a *counteralliance* on the other. Each side tried to become stronger than the other. In the 1800's Great Britain kept a balance of power in Europe by allying itself first with one side, then with the other.

Since World War II, a new power balance has been formed, based on three groups—the United States and western European nations, the Soviet

Union and eastern European Communist nations, and the People's Republic of China. The three powers compete for the friendship of the underdeveloped countries in Asia, Africa, and Latin America (so-called "third-world" nations). Many underdeveloped nations have vast resources of raw materials and manpower.

International relations today have been influenced by the United Nations. The United Nations serves as a meeting place where countries can argue their disagreements and sometimes find solutions that may avoid their going to war. The United Nations also tries to persuade countries to obey international law in their relations with one another.

Official relations among nations are carried on by *ambassadors* and their staffs of foreign service officers. An ambassador is an official representative of his or her government in a foreign country. Ambassadors must keep informed of the policies and decisions of their country's government. They must be able to explain their government's policies to officials of the foreign government. They must also be good at persuading the foreign government to agree with their country's policies. Ambassadors must be well informed about the country in which they are stationed. They must report to their government on the policies and actions of the foreign country. And they must be ready to advise their government in

any dealings it has with that country. Relations between countries are sometimes carried out by heads of government, as when the President of the United States meets with the leaders of other nations.

For further information on:
International Alliances, *see* COMMONWEALTH OF NATIONS, EUROPEAN COMMUNITY, NORTH ATLANTIC TREATY ORGANIZATION, ORGANIZATION OF AMERICAN STATES, WARSAW PACT.
International Diplomacy, *see* FOREIGN SERVICE.
International Organizations, *see* LEAGUE OF NATIONS, UNITED NATIONS.
International Relations and Economics, *see* COLONY, ECONOMICS, INTERNATIONAL TRADE, NATION.
Relations between Countries, *see* INTERNATIONAL LAW, TREATY, WAR.

INTERNATIONAL TRADE Every country engages in international trade. A country sells some things that it produces to other countries. Products sent out of the country are called *exports*. A country also buys products that it needs from other countries. Products brought into the country are called *imports*. International trade takes place because countries generally produce more of certain things than they need, and not enough of other things. For example, Japan is a leading manufacturer of automobiles. It exports cars and other

▲ *When fully loaded, a modern multi-cargo ship makes maximum use of its capacity.*

◄ *The flags of some of the European Community countries. The original six have now expanded to include twelve countries.*

The United States Patent Office has issued about four million patents for inventions, a number roughly equal to the total issued by the patent offices of Great Britain, Germany, and France combined.

▲ *This turbo-jet flying pack has hand controls for steering and adjusting power. This is an invention that has still to realize its full potential. So far, its use has been restricted to media events such as the 1984 Los Angeles Olympics opening ceremony and James Bond movies.*

goods to other nations. But Japan cannot raise enough food to feed its population, so it imports food from nations that raise great amounts of agricultural products.

Why do nations produce large amounts of some products and not enough of others? Nature is one reason. Oranges, for instance, grow best in hot climates. Some metals, such as copper, are found only in certain areas of the world. Each nation concentrates on the products it can produce best with the resources it has. A nation imports goods that it cannot produce at home, or that it can produce only at a higher cost than the import price. Some nations, such as the United States, are able to produce most of the things they need. But every country, no matter how wealthy, needs to do some trading. The United States must import items such as coffee, tea, natural rubber, sugar, and tropical fruits.

Trading nations try to keep a good *balance of payments*. The balance of payments is the comparison between the amount of money coming into a country when others pay for its exports, and the amount of money going out when a country buys imports. When a country exports more than it imports, more money comes into the country than goes out of it. This is considered a favorable balance of payments.

Governments sometimes set up *tariffs* (taxes on imports) or *quotas* (limits on the amount of goods that may be imported). Tariffs and quotas raise the prices of products coming into a country. The higher the prices on products, the less trade takes place. People will not buy the imports if they cost more than products made in their own country. Tariffs and quotas are usually set up by a government to protect the farmers and manufacturers of its own country. For example, if the United States puts a tariff on imported cars, the prices of these cars become higher than the

prices of U.S. cars. Since the American-made cars are then cheaper, people are more likely to buy them.

Some nations have joined together in "trading communities" in order to do away with tariffs and quotas and to promote free trade among the member nations. The European Community is a trading community in western Europe. Members of the Commonwealth of Nations also have trade agreements.

ALSO READ: EUROPEAN COMMUNITY, COMMONWEALTH OF NATIONS.

INTRODUCTION see MANNERS.

INVENTION Look around your home or classroom and observe the tools and other objects that you use every day. You will begin to see how much you depend on inventions in your daily life. The books you read in school would not have been possible without the invention of paper and ink—or of printing itself. Pencils, pens, typewriters, staplers, and pencil-sharpeners are also useful inventions. Both your school and home have electric lights and heating systems that came about through the work of inventors. At home you also have a refrigerator, telephone, radio, and other useful things. Countless other inventions are vital to industry, business, medicine, farming, and other fields.

An invention may be the creation of something completely new or an improvement of something made before. Many important inventions have resulted from the work of one hard-working individual. Inventors often owe much to discoveries and inventions made by others before them. For instance, James Watt invented the first workable steam engine, but his invention was based on earlier models built by others. Samuel F. B. Morse's telegraph, however, was a completely original invention.

▲ *Thomas Alva Edison, one of America's greatest inventors. The incandescent light bulb and the phonograph were among his many inventions.*

At times, two or more inventors, working independently, have come up with the same invention. For example, Elisha Gray and Alexander Graham Bell both applied for a patent on the telephone on the same day in 1876. (A *patent* gives an inventor the legal rights to his invention and forbids anyone else to copy it or claim to have invented it.) Gray made his application a few hours later than Bell, so Bell received credit for the invention.

Many modern inventions have been created not by one person, but by many people working together as a team. The atom bomb, for instance, was developed during World War II by a large group of scientists and technicians. Today, research teams in government, industrial, and university laboratories work hard to create new inventions or to improve existing inventions.

Not all inventors have been scientists or experts in their fields. Ordinary people have invented useful objects. Some inventions have even come about by accident. Charles Goodyear, the inventor of vulcanized rubber, was a hardware salesman with no formal education. He was trying to find a way to treat natural rubber so that it would not become brittle when cold, or soft and sticky when hot. He made hundreds of un-

SOME IMPORTANT INVENTIONS

Year	Invention	Inventor(s)	Nationality
c. 1447	Movable type printing	Johannes Gutenberg	German
c. 1615	Clinical thermometer	Sanctorius	Italian
1608	Telescope	Hans Lippershey	Dutch
1642	Adding machine	Blaise Pascal	French
1705	Steam engine	Thomas Newcomen	British
1769	Steam engine for power	James Watt	British
1783	Parachute	Louis S. Lenormand	French
1793	Cotton gin	Eli Whitney	American
1800	Electric battery	Alessandro Volta	Italian
1804	Steam locomotive	Richard Trevithick	British
1807	First commercial steamship	Robert Fulton	American
1816	Phosphorus match	François Derosne	French
1816–1827	Photography	Joseph Nicéphore Niepce	French
1819	Stethoscope	René Laënnec	French
1821	Electric motor	Michael Faraday	British
1837	Telegraph	Samuel F. B. Morse	American
1846	Sewing machine	Elias Howe	American
1852	Elevator	Elisha Otis	American
1866	Dynamite	Alfred Nobel	Swedish
1867	Typewriter	Christopher Sholes Samuel Soule Carlos Glidden	American
1876	Telephone	Alexander Graham Bell	American
1877	Internal combustion engine (4-cycle)	Nikolaus Otto	German
1884	Fountain pen	Lewis E. Waterman	American
1885	Gasoline automobile	Karl Benz, Otto Daimler	German
1888	Kodak camera	George Eastman	American
1891	Zipper	Whitcomb L. Judson	American
1893	Motion picture machine	Thomas Edison	American
1895	X-ray machine	Wilhelm Roentgen	German
1896	Wireless telegraph	Guglielmo Marconi	Italian
1903	Airplane (with motor)	Orville and Wilbur Wright	American
1907	Radio vacuum tube	Lee De Forest	American
1911	Air conditioning	Willis Carrier	American
1923–1928	Television	Vladimir Zworykin John L. Baird Philo T. Farnsworth	American British American
1926	Rocket engine	Robert Goddard	American
1926	Aerosol spray	Eric Rotheim	Norwegian
1928	Jet engine	Frank Whittle	British
1935	Radar Nylon	Robert Watson-Watt Wallace H. Carothers	British American
1938	Xerography	Chester Carlson	American
1939	Helicopter	Sikorsky	American
1942	Atomic reactor	Enrico Fermi	American
1944	Digital computer Ballpoint pen	Howard Aiken Lazlo Biro	American Argentine
1947	Polaroid camera	Edwin Land	American
1948	Transistor	John Bardeen William Shockley Walter Brattain	American
1955	Optical fibers Air cushion vehicle	Dr. Narinder Kapary Christopher Cockerell	British British
1960	Masers and Lasers	Charles H. Townes Theodore H. Maiman	American
1966	Artificial heart	Michael DeBakey	American

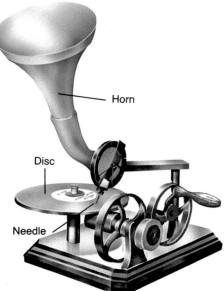

▲ *The gramophone, which played flat discs rather than cylinders as Edison's machine did, was invented by a German, Emile Berliner, in 1887.*

▼ *A modern invention—the industrial robot. These machines, with mechanical arms ending in handlike gripping devices, were developed in the 1960's for performing routine tasks in factories.*

successful experiments, mixing rubber with different materials. Then one day in 1839, Goodyear accidentally dropped some rubber, which he had treated with sulfur, into the fire. The heat gave the mixture the elastic quality he wanted. This method of treating rubber, *vulcanization*, is still the basis of rubber manufacturing.

The Process of Invention Many inventions have been brought about by economic, social, or military needs. For example, the invention of the cotton gin by Eli Whitney in 1793 helped agriculture in the South because this machine could remove the seeds from cotton as fast as 50 laborers working by hand.

Social needs have inspired the development of new medical instruments and drugs in the fight against disease. Roentgen's discovery of X rays in 1895, for instance, resulted in great advances in the detection and treatment of disease.

Wars have always stimulated invention, both destructive and constructive. The Civil War, for example, produced the Gatling gun, the forerunner of the machine gun. But at the same time it established the widespread use of the telegraph as a means of fast communication.

History of Inventions The earliest inventions were tools and weapons that helped people to build shelters and obtain food. Prehistoric people chipped stones with other stones to make simple hammers and axes. They also shaped stones into crude knives and spear points for hunting. These stone tools later gave way to tools made of bronze and iron, as people learned to use metals. Early people also learned to make clothing, first from animal skins and later from plant materials. They invented plows and learned how to plant and harvest grains and other foods. They also dug out logs to make crude boats.

One of the most important of early inventions was the wheel. The wheel made carts and wagons possible, as well as inventions such as the potter's wheel and the waterwheel. The waterwheel, believed to have been invented by the Romans about 100 B.C., was a large wheel with paddles attached to the rim. The wheel was put under a waterfall so that the wheel turned when the water struck the paddles. The turning axle of the wheel, attached to a machine, gave the machine power to operate. Waterwheels were long used for such jobs as grinding grain and pumping water. Windmills came into use in Europe in the 1100's. Just as the waterwheel used moving water as a source of power, the windmill used the force of moving air.

Most inventions have been welcomed by society. But some have encountered resistance, especially when new technology has threatened jobs. During the Industrial Revolution, some workers attacked and smashed the new machines that they felt were depriving them of work. Even today society has to deal with problems arising from new technology. Microchip technology, for example, is reducing the need for people in many factories and offices. And the side effects of inventions such as the automobile, which produces pollution, can be harmful.

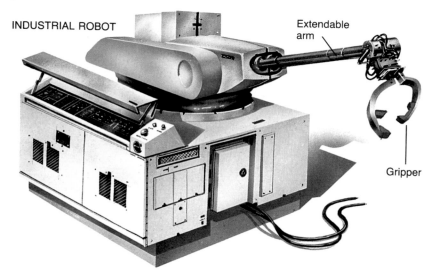

INDUSTRIAL ROBOT

Extendable arm

Gripper

For further information on:

Inventions, *see* AIR CONDITIONING, AIR CUSHION VEHICLE, AIRPLANE, AIRSHIP, AUTOMOBILE, BICYCLE, BODY SCANNER, CALCULATOR, CAMERA, CASSETTE AND CARTRIDGES, CLOCKS AND WATCHES, COMPACT DISC, COMPUTER, ELEVATORS AND ESCALATORS, EXPLOSIVES, FIBER OPTICS, GEIGER COUNTER, GUNS AND RIFLES, GYROSCOPE, HEATING, HELICOPTER, HOLOGRAPHY, HYDROFOIL, JET PROPULSION, LASER AND MASER, LENS, LIE DETECTOR, LIGHTING, LOCKS AND KEYS, MATCH, MICROSCOPE, MOTION PICTURE, PAPER, PARACHUTE, PARTICLE ACCELERATOR, PENS AND PENCILS, PHOTOCOPIER, PHOTOGRAPHY, PLASTIC, PRINTING, RADAR, RADIO, RECORDING, REFRIGERATION, ROCKET, RUBBER, SATELLITE, SEWING MACHINE, SNOWMOBILE, SUBMARINE, SYNTHETIC, TELECOMMUNICATIONS, TELEGRAPH, TELEPHONE, TELESCOPE, TELEVISION, THERMOMETER, X RAY.

Inventors, *see* BAIRD, JOHN L.; BELL, ALEXANDER GRAHAM; EDISON, THOMAS ALVA; FARADAY, MICHAEL; FERMI, ENRICO; FRANKLIN, BENJAMIN; FULTON, ROBERT; HOWE, ELIAS; GALILEO; GODDARD, ROBERT H.; GUTENBERG, JOHANNES; LEONARDO DA VINCI; MC CORMICK, CYRUS; MARCONI, GUGLIELMO; MORSE, SAMUEL F.B.; NEWTON, ISAAC; PASCAL, BLAISE; STEPHENSON, GEORGE; VON BRAUN, WERNHER; WATT, JAMES; WHITNEY, ELI; WRIGHT BROTHERS; ZWORYKIN, VLADIMIR.

General, *see* INDUSTRIAL REVOLUTION, PATENTS AND COPYRIGHTS.

INVERTEBRATE see ANIMAL KINGDOM.

INVESTMENT see STOCKS AND BONDS.

ION see ATOM.

IOWA Iowa reputedly took its name from the Iowa or Ioway Indians, one of several tribes that lived in various parts of the state before the white settlers came. The Indians liked this prairie region. They raised vegetables in the rich soil and hunted great herds of buffalo on the plains.

The Land and Climate Iowa lies in the plains that curve west and south of the Great Lakes. Minnesota is north of its straight northern boundary. Missouri is south of its almost-straight southern boundary. Its western boundary line is not straight at all. It is formed by the Missouri River and the Big Sioux River, which flows into the Missouri. Nebraska and South Dakota are Iowa's western neighbors. Its eastern boundary is wavy, too. It is formed by the Mississippi River, which separates Iowa from Illinois and Wisconsin.

Most of Iowa is a gently rolling plain. The state is highest in the northwest. It is lowest in the southeast. But it really slopes in *two* directions. The rivers show that it does. The Des Moines River and the other rivers in the eastern two-thirds of Iowa flow southeast toward the Mississippi. The rivers in the western third of the state flow southwest.

Iowa is wonderful farming country. No other state has so much top-grade soil. Most of the Iowa region was covered with tall prairie grass for hundreds of years. The long grass roots added to the plant food in the soil as they decayed. Iowa also has a very good climate for crops. There is usually enough rain for the crops during the six warm months. It is brought by winds from the south. The hot sunshine of long summer days helps the crops ripen. Winter winds from the north give Iowa bright days and frosty nights.

History Prehistoric Indians called Mound Builders once lived in Iowa.

▲ *Theodore Maiman, the American scientist who invented the laser in 1960. The first laser produced a beam of red light.*

St. Anthony's Chapel in Festina, Iowa, built in 1885, is said to be the smallest church in the world. It has only four pews.

Almost 80,000 Iowans fought in the Civil War, and about 13,000 of them were killed.

▶ *The Governor's Mansion in Des Moines. Built in 1869, it has recently been restored. It was given to the state in 1970.*

Iowa's first capital was Burlington, but the government was moved to Iowa City in 1839 and finally to Des Moines in 1857.

They built large mounds of earth as burial places or as bases for houses and temples. Most of their mounds are cone-shaped. But some, called *effigy* mounds, are in the form of huge birds or beasts. These interesting mounds can be seen in Effigy Mounds National Monument, near the town of Marquette on the Mississippi River.

The mounds were already old when the first white people arrived. Two French explorers, Louis Joliet and Father Jacques Marquette, came down the Mississippi River in canoes and landed on the Iowa shore on June 25, 1673. La Salle, another French explorer, later traveled down the Mississippi and claimed the entire area drained by the river for France.

Several Indian tribes played important parts in the history of this region. One was the warlike Sioux. Another was the Sauk. These and other tribes, including the Fox, Iowa, and Winnebago, occupied most of the state until the 1800's.

Iowa was a small part of the huge French territory called Louisiana. France let Spain control the Louisiana Territory for a time. But the persons who entered the Iowa region during the the 1700's were French.

The first one to start a settlement was Julien Dubuque, a French-Canadian pioneer from Quebec. He asked the Fox Indians to let him mine lead near the Mississippi. The chiefs granted his request in 1788. Dubuque and the Indians became good friends. Today, a city and a county in Iowa have his name. They mark the place where his trading post, farm, and mines were once located.

The United States bought the whole territory of Louisiana from France in 1803. Americans found, as the French had, that the Iowa region was rich in fur-bearing animals. The American Fur Company started trading posts there to buy furs from the Indians. Keokuk (in Iowa's southwestern corner) is one of several towns that began as trading posts.

The Indians liked traders who treated them fairly. They liked being able to exchange furs for wool blankets and other goods. But some settlers cheated the Indians to get their land. For this reason, a number of tribes sided with Great Britain in the War of 1812. Their leader was Black Hawk, a Sauk chief. Black Hawk made peace with the white Americans after the war. But unjust treatment led him to fight them again in the Black Hawk War of 1832. He was defeated. During the years that followed, almost all the Indians were pushed out of Iowa.

Iowa became a state in 1846. By this time, a flood of settlers was pouring in. They came by wagon from the East and South. Most of them had oxen. They had heard that horses and mules weren't strong enough to pull plows through the thick prairie sod (grass-covered earth). The early farmers there became known as *sod busters*.

Once the sod was broken, all was well. The farmers then had excellent cropland. News of the fertile soil spread around the world. Many European farmers came to Iowa. Most came from Germany, Norway, Sweden, Denmark, the Netherlands, and Ireland. The Amanites, a religious

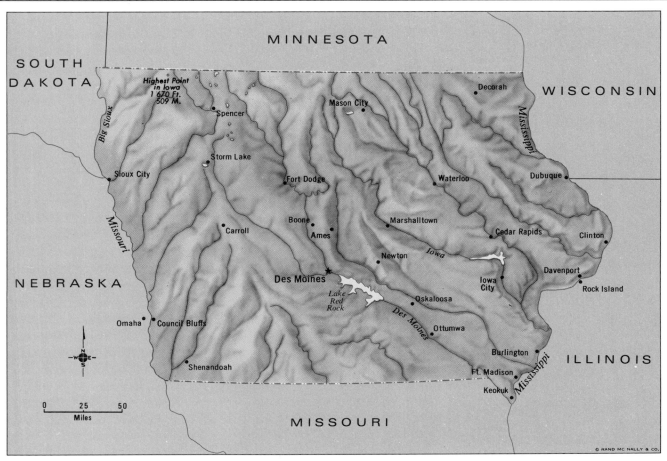

IOWA

Capital and largest city
Des Moines (191,000 people)

Area
56,290 square miles (145,780 sq. km)
Rank: 25th

Population
2,834,000
Rank: 29th

Statehood
December 28, 1846
(29th state admitted)

Principal river
Des Moines River

Highest point
Ocheyedan Mound
1,670 feet (509 m)

Motto
Our liberties we prize and our rights we will maintain.

Song
"Song of Iowa"

Famous people
James K. Van Allen, Buffalo Bill Cody, Herbert Hoover, Henry Wallace, Meredith Willson, Grant Wood.

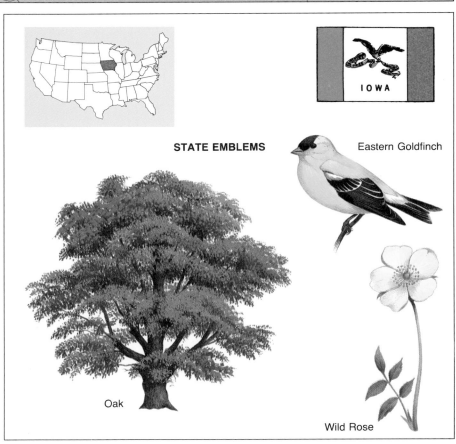

STATE EMBLEMS

Eastern Goldfinch

Oak

Wild Rose

▲ *Iowa has many fine lake resort areas, especially in the northern part of the state. In this region, sailing is a popular pastime.*

group from Germany, founded seven villages near Iowa City in 1855. Some of the villagers there still produce old German handicrafts. Many Dutch families settled in Pella in southeastern Iowa. Their descendants dress up in traditional Dutch costumes each spring for the annual Tulip Festival. Historical museums in Decorah, in the northeast, show how the early Norwegian farm families of this region lived and worked.

Iowans at Work Iowa is an important farming state. Agriculture brings the state more than seven billion dollars' worth of business every year. This makes Iowa second only to California in the value of its agricultural products. Iowa is the nation's leading producer of corn. Soybeans are important, too. But livestock brings in more money than crops do. Much corn is not sold. The farmers who raise it feed it to hogs and cattle instead.

Although Iowa is a leading agricultural state, it is also a manufacturing state. Machinery is the number-one product of Iowa's manufacturing industry. Much of it is farm machinery. Food products are second in value. Both agricultural and industrial products are exhibited at the Iowa State Fair, held in Des Moines every summer.

ALSO READ: GREAT LAKES, LOUISIANA PURCHASE, PRAIRIE.

IRAN Iran is about four times the size of California and has more than one and a half times as many people. Many Iranians are farmers, living in villages in mountain valleys. Others live and work in large cities, where modern buildings stand next to old mud-walled houses and *mosques* (Muslim temples of worship). Wandering tribes in the deserts and mountains herd goats, sheep, and camels, whose wool and hair are used to make the famous Persian carpets. Most Iranians are Muslims.

Iran's northern boundaries are the Soviet Union and the Caspian Sea. The Gulf of Oman and the Persian Gulf lap its southern shores. Iraq lies to the west, and Afghanistan and Pakistan lie to the east. Tehran, the largest city, is the capital.

Iran is mainly a plateau, 4,000 feet (1,219 m) above sea level, surrounded by mountain ranges. A vast desert stretches about 800 miles (1,300 km) across the central part of the country. Much of Iran receives 10 inches (25 cm) or less of rainfall each year. However, the area near the Caspian Sea receives up to 50 inches (127 cm).

Most of the land suitable for farming is irrigated. Wheat, barley, and rice are grown. Other crops are tobacco, tea, dates, apricots, sugar beets, cotton, and corn. The country has coal, lead, copper, chromite, and iron. However, oil is Iran's most important natural resource.

IRAN

Capital City: Tehran (6,000,000 people).
Area: 636,296 square miles (1,647,879 sq. km).
Population: 51,000,000.
Government: Islamic republic.
Natural Resources: Oil and natural gas, iron ore, coal.
Export Products: Oil and oil products, natural gas, cotton.
Unit of Money: Rial.
Official Language: Farsi (Persian).

The country's industries depend upon agricultural production and natural resources. Silk, cotton, and wool are woven. Hides, tobacco, and sugar beets are processed. Oil is refined, and copper is smelted.

The Iranians are descendants of the Medes and Persians. These people came to the area of present-day Iran about 900 years before the birth of Christ. Cyrus the Great, an ancient statesman and warrior, conquered the Medes and Persians in about 550 B.C. He united the area now called the Middle East and built it into the Persian Empire.

Alexander the Great, a Greek general, conquered the Persian Empire in 331 B.C. Other invaders came and went, including Arabs, Mongols, and Turks. Great Britain and Russia also fought to control Iran during the 1800's.

Riza Shah Pahlavi ruled Iran as shah (king) from 1925 to 1941. He made reforms in transportation, government, industry, education, and the army. He demanded that parliament pass new laws, including women's voting rights. After his abdication (giving up the throne), his son, Mohammed Riza Pahlavi, became shah and sought to make Iran a military power. In 1979, the shah was deposed in a revolution under Ayatollah Khomeini, who set up an Islamic republic. A long war with neighboring Iraq began in 1980, causing heavy casualties on both sides. It ended in 1988.

ALSO READ: ALEXANDER THE GREAT, ISLAM, MIDDLE EAST, PERSIA.

IRAQ The word "Iraq" comes from an Arabic word meaning "origin." The name probably refers to the fact that this fertile valley between the Tigris and Euphrates rivers may have been the birthplace of civilization. Iraq is bounded on the north by Turkey, on the east by Iran, on the south by Saudi Arabia, and on the west by Syria and Jordan. The only outlet to the sea is a narrow strip of coast on

There are about 20,000 mosques (Muslim churches) in Iran.

▼ *The domes and slender minarets of Muslim mosques dominate the skyline in many Iranian towns and cities. These are in the city of Mashad.*

IRAQ

Capital City: Baghdad (3,400,000 people).
Area: 167,925 square miles (434,892 sq. km).
Population: 17,600,000.
Government: Republic with military government (Revolutionary Command Council).
Natural Resources: Oil and natural gas.
Export Products: Oil, dates, barley.
Unit of Money: Dinar.
Official Language: Arabic.

Where Iraq's two great rivers come together is said to be the site of the Garden of Eden.

▼ *The madrasa Mulaniyah in Baghdad. Madrasas were teaching colleges; old Baghdad was famous as a center of learning.*

the Persian Gulf. The ancient city of Baghdad is the capital. (See the map with the article on the MIDDLE EAST.)

The climate in Iraq varies according to location. The northern part of the country has cold winters and cool summers. The central area has short, cool winters and long, hot summers. The country receives 10 inches (25 cm) of rainfall or less each year.

About 95 percent of the Iraqi people are Muslims. Many live in and around cities, working in businesses and factories. Others are farmers and herders in small villages and towns. Some *nomadic* (wandering) shepherds live in the deserts and mountains. Their leaders, called *sheiks*, are sometimes wealthy and powerful.

Iraq's most valuable natural resource is oil. Much natural gas, sulfur, gypsum, and salt are found, too.

Iraq is the world's leading producer of dates. Cotton, tobacco, fruits, and grain crops are also grown. Important industries include the manufacture of glass, cigarettes and other tobacco products, vegetable oils, soap, woolen textiles, brick, and tile.

Records of civilization in Mesopotamia go back 6,000 years. The area was conquered by Persia in 538 B.C., and then invaded and ruled by several other conquerors. Iraq was under Turkish rule from 1638 until World War I, when it came under British control. Iraq became independent in 1932. Political disputes and military takeovers have marked Iraq's years as an independent state. Since 1968, the country has had a military government. A revolt by the Kurds, a Muslim group in the north, was put down in 1975. Iraq began a long war against Iran in 1980, seeking control of the Shatt-al-Arab waterway that divides both countries. The war ended in 1988.

ALSO READ: ISLAM, MESOPOTAMIA, MIDDLE EAST, TIGRIS AND EUPHRATES RIVERS.

IRELAND Ireland is a land of wild seacoasts and misty rolling hills—so green that it is sometimes called the Emerald Isle. Whitewashed cottages with thatched roofs dot the countryside. The Irish people are known for their wit, imagination, spirit, and hospitality.

Ireland lies west of Great Britain, between the Irish Sea and the Atlantic Ocean. The island is divided into two parts. Most of the island is the independent Republic of Ireland, often known as Eire (the Irish name for the whole island). The northeastern region, Northern Ireland (Ulster), is part of the United Kingdom. The capital of the Republic is the ancient city of Dublin. (See the map with the article on BRITISH ISLES.)

A gentle region of hills, *loughs* (lakes), and rivers stretches across central Ireland to the west coast. Here, massive granite cliffs and rugged headlands face the storms of the Atlantic Ocean. The Shannon River, the longest river in the British Isles, flows southward across central Ireland. The climate of the island is moderate and moist.

The Irish people are descended mainly from Celtic tribes that settled in Ireland more than 2,000 years ago. The Irish encourage the use of the ancient Celtic language, *Gaelic*. Most people also speak English, which is spoken with an accent called a *brogue*. The major religion in Ireland is Roman Catholicism.

Ireland has few natural resources. Farming and food processing are the most important industries. Tourism earns much money for the country, too. Visitors love the friendly people, good fishing, quaint countryside, and ancient castles. Irish dairy products, woolen goods, *stout* (a heavy, dark beer), and whiskey are exported to

other parts of the world. Homes and small industries in Ireland burn peat (a soft form of coal) from the Irish bogs for fuel. Peat diggers, with their ponies and carts, and farmers with their donkeys are familiar sights.

Saint Patrick, the patron saint of Ireland, converted the Irish to Christianity in the 400's. After the barbarians overran Europe in the 500's and 600's, devout Irish monks kept Christianity alive. They copied down the religious scriptures by hand in beautifully decorated books, such as the famous *Book of Kells*. Ancient Celtic folklore survived in ballads and legends. Later, Irish writers sometimes used these legends as themes for their stories and poems. Many modern Irish authors, including William Butler Yeats, James Joyce, Oscar Wilde, and George Bernard Shaw, have become famous throughout the world.

The high kings of Ireland ruled from a great palace at Tara, near

▲ *Ireland still has many small farms with fields bounded by hedgerows. Here, the grass has been cut and stacked. It is dried to make hay.*

About one-seventh of the whole surface of Ireland is covered by bogs—places where peat has been formed or is now being formed. Peat is a spongy mass of vegetable matter that is found in layers many feet thick. It is said that an inch or two of peat forms every year in Ireland's bogs. When it is dried, peat can be burned as fuel.

IRELAND

Capital City: Dublin (500,000 people).
Area: 27,136 square miles (70,276 sq. km).
Population: 3,700,000.
Government: Republic.
Natural Resources: Peat, lead, zinc.
Export Products: Machinery and transport equipment, live animals and food.
Unit of Money: Pound.
Official Languages: Irish, English.

▲ *Fishing is a popular pastime as well as an industry on the west coast of Ireland. These fishermen are trying their luck near Galway Bay.*

▼ *A huge open-pit iron ore mine in Western Australia, where the ore is scooped up from the surface of the earth.*

Dublin, in the Middle Ages. In the 1100's, the first English invasions began from the east. In the 1500's, English settlers began to seize land throughout Ireland. These Protestant settlers brutally persecuted the Roman Catholic Irish. The Irish had no political rights and were forced to live in poverty on the poorest land. Their diet was mainly potatoes. In the 1840's, a disease destroyed the potato crop for several years and millions of Irish people died of starvation. Others left to go to the United States.

In 1916, a revolution known as the Easter Rebellion broke out. It was led by a group of Irish patriots called the *Sinn Féin* ("We Ourselves"). In 1949, Britain finally recognized the independence of the Republic of Ireland but kept control of the northern counties. Conflict in the north between Irish nationalists and Unionists, who wanted the north to stay part of Britain, led to much bloodshed. In 1985, the Republic and Britain tried to solve the problems in the north by agreeing to set up a joint commission to give the Republic an advisory role in ruling the north. But the Unionists strongly opposed this plan, and the turmoil continued in Northern Ireland.

ALSO READ: BRITISH ISLES, ENGLAND, ENGLISH HISTORY, UNITED KINGDOM.

IRON see VITAMINS AND MINERALS.

IRON AND STEEL Thousands of years ago, people used tools made of stone, copper, or bronze. Then people began to find pieces of iron meteorites. They discovered that the iron was heavier and harder than stone, copper, or bronze. By hammering the iron, they could shape it into knives, arrowheads, and spear points, and it could even be made into jewelry. The iron was believed to have magic powers because it came from the heavens.

In some ancient languages, the word for iron meant "metal from the sky." Iron was considered more valuable than gold, silver, copper, or bronze.

Copper, gold, silver, and some other metals were obtained when people learned that rocks of certain colors, or *ores*, were changed by fire. Fire caused the metal ore in the rocks to melt. The melting of ore to obtain metal is called *smelting*. The metals are poured off and cooled so they would harden. Then the hardened metals were made into tools.

No one knows when or where people first discovered that they could make iron by smelting iron ore. The discovery was certainly made several thousand years ago, possibly in several different areas. The Bible mentions iron and other metals. Iron was used in China, Egypt, the Middle East, and Europe long before the time of Christ.

After it was discovered in large quantities, iron was no longer considered so valuable as some of the rarer metals. Iron ore is now mined in most countries of the world. One of the largest iron ore regions in the United States is in Minnesota, near Lake Superior. Most of the high-grade ore has been mined, but a method has been developed to process a low-grade ore called *taconite*.

The iron mines in Minnesota are *open-pit* mines. This type of mine is used when the ore is near the surface of the ground. Big loads of ore are scooped up from the open ground by giant steam shovels, to be hauled away for smelting. This digging makes a huge open pit. In other iron ore ranges, the ore is sometimes deep underground. A tunnel, or *shaft*, is dug downward into the ground until the ore is reached. Miners go down into the shaft and dig out the ore, which is then hoisted to the surface.

For many years, iron ore was smelted on a fire of charcoal. The iron had to be hammered and reheated several times before it was free of *impurities* (the other materials in the ore). The first *blast furnaces* were made in Europe in the 1300's. A blast furnace is a tall, cylinder-shaped building with a hearth inside, on which the iron ore is smelted. Modern blast furnaces may be over 200 feet (60 m) high. Blasts of heated air make the fire so hot that most of the impurities are burned away. The melted iron sinks to the bottom of the furnace and the impurities are collected as *slag* or burned off as gases. In the 1700's, people discovered that *coke* (a by-product of coal) smelted iron much faster than charcoal. Coke has been used for smelting ever since. Crushed limestone is also added to the fire in a blast furnace. Chemicals in the limestone help to purify the iron. After the iron has been smelted in a blast furnace, it is poured into bar-shaped molds, or *pigs*. It then hardens into *pig iron*. The pigs are shipped to a *foundry*, where they are reheated and *cast* (poured into molds) to make iron products. This type of iron is called *cast iron*. Cast iron is brittle, hard, and heavy.

To make a different kind of iron, the pigs are reheated and mixed with a glasslike sand. The iron is then cooled. After it hardens, it can be put between rollers and squeezed into desired sizes. This kind of iron is called *wrought iron*. It can be bent or twisted without breaking. Wrought iron is used to make such things as iron gates, garden furniture, and pipelines.

In the 1850's, different discoveries made by three men, working separately, showed how iron could be cheaply and easily made into *steel*. The men were William Kelley, an American, Robert F. Mushet, a Scot, and Sir Henry Bessemer, an Englishman. Their inventions created the steel industry.

Steel is an *alloy*. An alloy is a mixture of two or more metals. Steel is made by mixing melted iron with measured amounts of other sub-

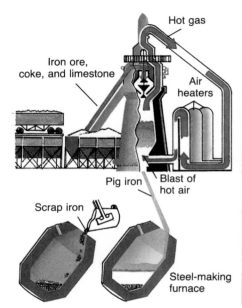
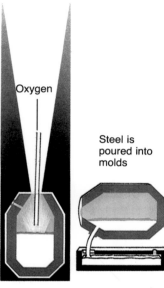

stances, such as carbon, manganese, chromium, tungsten, molybdenum, and nickel. Different alloys make different kinds of steel. For example, *stainless steel* is mostly an alloy of steel and chromium. But all steel begins with iron ore. Steel is much stronger than iron and can be shaped more accurately.

Today an increasingly important way of smelting iron ore is in the electric furnace. Long carbon rods, or *electrodes*, able to carry large electric currents, are lowered into a chamber containing the iron ore and limestone. They are positioned within a few inches of the ore. When the power is turned on, an electric arc jumps across the air gap. This creates intense heat that melts the metal and burns out the impurities. The quality of the steel produced is easier to control with this method.

The spray process of steelmaking is a method still in the experimental stages. In this process, molten pig iron is sprayed through a current of oxygen and a spray of limestone powder. Impurities are burned out or combined with the limestone.

The United States, the Soviet Union, Japan, West Germany, China, France, Italy, and Great Britain are the world's leading producers of iron and steel. Great quantities of this

▲ *Making steel. Iron ore is mixed with coke and limestone, and the mixture is heated in a blast furnace to make pig iron. Pig iron has too much carbon to make steel, so the extra carbon is burned off by blowing oxygen over it. The molten steel is then poured into molds to make steel blocks.*

▲ *An ingot being rolled into the shape of a slab, a rectangular piece of steel. Some ingots are shaped into blooms or billets, which are squared pieces of steel.*

▲ *The Coalbrookdale Iron-works, England, painted in 1805.*

Have you ever wondered why iron turns red when it is heated? When it is heated to about 1500°F (800°C) the atoms in the iron vibrate and send out waves that we see as a dull red. As the temperature increases, the atoms vibrate faster and the iron turns bright red and finally white-hot, before it begins to melt.

iron and steel are sold to other countries that do not have enough iron mines or steel mills to meet their own needs. Iron and steel are used in the building of skyscrapers, automobiles, steamships, airplanes, rockets and space ships, bicycles, railroad tracks, trains, toys, computers, knives, guns, and thousands of other goods. The iron and steel industries are among the most important in the world.

ALSO READ: ALLOY, INDUSTRIAL REVOLUTION, METAL, MINES AND MINING.

IROQUOIS INDIANS In part of what is now New York State, five Indian tribes (the Mohawk, Oneida, Onondaga, Cayuga, and Seneca) united to form the Iroquois Confederacy, or the Five Nations. The life of the Iroquois was highly organized and culturally advanced.

The Iroquois lived in villages defended by *palisade fences*, or fences of tall, pointed pieces of wood tied closely together. They lived in long wooden structures called "long houses." Several related families lived in each house. Each family had its own part of the long house.

The Iroquois grew corn (*maize*),

squash, and beans. The women of the tribes tended the fields and picked wild fruits and vegetables. Maple sugar was also enjoyed by the Iroquois. Collected elm bark was used for covering the walls and roofs of the long houses and for making containers. The men and boys went on hunting and fishing expeditions.

Women had a very important place among the Iroquois. The head of each family was an elderly woman. Women owned the long houses, the fields, and the crops. An Iroquois traced his or her ancestors through the mother's family. The matrons at the head of the most important Iroquois families were responsible for choosing the chiefs, or *sachems*, who sat in the tribal council. The sachems governed the tribes, but if they did not govern wisely the women dismissed them.

Religion was an important part of Iroquois life. Any man or woman who was thought to have magical powers could become a priest. The major religious festival was celebrated in midwinter. Ceremonies at this time were supposed to encourage the growth of the new year's crops. The members of the False Face Society

▼ *An early photograph of an Iroquois family on the Brantford Reserve in Ontario, Canada.*

danced, wearing frightening masks. These masks were believed to destroy evil spirits.

The Iroquois believed in justice, healthful living, and cooperation and respect between people.

ALSO READ: FIVE NATIONS.

IRRIGATION For thousands of years, farmers have taken water from rivers to make up for lack of rain. At first, farmers simply dug narrow channels from the river to their fields. This was irrigation, but it had limitations. The irrigated fields had to be downhill from the river and close to it, because there were no pumps to carry the water uphill or over long distances. These problems have been solved by modern irrigation methods.

Irrigation plays an important part in agriculture today. In the United States, irrigation makes it possible for farmers to use about 40 million acres (16 million hectares) of land normally too dry for farming. The Columbia, Sacramento, San Joaquin, and Missouri rivers supply water for some of the largest irrigation systems in the United States. Other large systems are along the Nile River in Egypt, the Yellow River in China, the Indus River in Pakistan, the Ganges and Brahmaputra rivers in India, and the Tigris and Euphrates rivers in Iraq.

The pumps of a modern irrigation system can move millions of gallons of water a day. Some irrigation systems take water from underground wells. But most systems get water from rivers. In this case, a dam is built and the water is taken from the lake formed behind the dam.

Pumps carry water from the river into canals or concrete channels. Special tunnels are dug to carry the water under hills and mountains. Along the way are pumping stations that keep the water moving over long distances. Smaller canals, called *feeders*, branch

off from the main canal, and *laterals*, still smaller canals, branch off from the feeders.

There are several ways of bringing the water to the growing plants. Water may be allowed to flow from the laterals by gravity through the plowed furrows in which the crops are growing. In *underbedding*, the plants are grown on rows of small hills, and the water flows along the rows. The water seeps down to the roots of the plants. Sometimes a whole field is simply flooded at regular intervals.

Rows of sprinklers may be built in a field. The water is pumped through them from a central source and "rains" on the crops.

ALSO READ: AGRICULTURE, CANAL, DAM, PUMP.

▲ *Irrigation has made the desert bloom in Egypt. Here, an ox turns a wheel, raising pots of water from a large irrigation ditch to a smaller one. Methods such as this have been used for thousands of years.*

◄ *Today's farmer is greatly assisted by tractors to plow the fields and modern irrigation methods to water them. The system shown here involves pumping water at high pressure through a network of sprinklers.*

▲ *Washington Irving, writer and traveler, whose stories are read today in many parts of the world.*

▲ *Isabella and Ferdinand receive Christopher Columbus after his first voyage to America.*

IRVING, WASHINGTON (1783–1859) Washington Irving has been called the "Father of American Literature." He was the first important fiction writer in the United States and one of the first American authors to use the short-story form. His humorous stories and other writings won him fame in Europe as well as at home.

Irving was born in New York City. As a young man, he began a career as a lawyer. But he preferred writing and soon began to publish amusing little articles and essays. He published a humorous *History of New York* in 1809, under the made-up name Diedrich Knickerbocker. This book poked fun at history and at American government.

Irving traveled to Europe in 1815 for his family's business. Money troubles caused the business to fail a few years later, and Irving turned to writing as a full-time occupation. His next work was *The Sketch Book*, which included his two most popular stories—"The Legend of Sleepy Hollow" and "Rip Van Winkle." Both these stories were based on old legends that Irving had heard from Dutch-Americans in New York. "The Legend of Sleepy Hollow" is the tale of a timid schoolmaster, Ichabod Crane, and his terrifying meeting with the Headless Horseman. "Rip Van Winkle" is the story of a man who falls asleep for 20 years in the Catskill Mountains of New York. He wakes up after the American Revolution and finds that life in his town has changed completely.

Irving was appointed U.S. minister to Spain and was sent to Madrid in 1826. There he wrote several books, including a biography of Christopher Columbus. He later served as a diplomat in England, and again in Spain. He returned to America in 1846 and retired to Sunnyside, his country home on the Hudson River in Tarrytown, New York.

ISABELLA AND FERDINAND Spain became a strong nation under the rule of Queen Isabella (1451–1504) and King Ferdinand (1452–1516). In the early 1400's, Spain was a group of kingdoms. In 1469, at the age of 17, Ferdinand of the kingdom of Aragon married Isabella of Castile. She was just 18. Their marriage combined the two largest kingdoms in Spain. Isabella was a strong queen. She wanted to drive the Moors out of Spain. The Moors were Arabs who had come over to Spain from Africa. The Moors were forced to give up their last stronghold in the south, Granada, in 1492. In that same year, Isabella and Ferdinand gave Christopher Columbus the money he needed to make his first voyage in search of a westward route to India.

Isabella and Ferdinand wanted all of Spain to be Roman Catholic. They supported the Inquisition—special courts that tried anyone suspected of not believing the teachings of the Roman Catholic Church.

Ferdinand was a good soldier and good at negotiating with other leaders. He brought all of the land south of the Pyrenees mountains, except Portugal, under control of Spain. He also conquered Naples, Italy, and the islands of Corsica and Sardinia.

ALSO READ: COLUMBUS, CHRISTOPHER; SPAIN; SPANISH HISTORY.

ISLAM Islam is one of the world's great religions. Its greatest prophet (religious proclaimer) was an Arabian named Muhammad, who lived from about A.D. 570 to 632. The people who believe in Islam are called *Muslims*, or *Moslems*. Today, there are almost 600 million Muslims throughout the world. Most of them live in the Middle East, Africa, and Asia.

Islam in Arabic means "peace, purity, and obedience to God." According to Muslim belief, Muhammad saw the angel Gabriel in a vision. Gabriel told Muhammad that he was to be God's messenger to teach the words of God to the world. Those words became the holy writings of Islam, the book called the *Koran*.

Muhammad lived in Mecca, a great Arabian trading city. At that time, the Arab tribes worshiped many gods. Muhammad preached that there was only one God. He urged the people to give up their wicked ways and live virtuous lives. The people of Mecca did not wish to change their ways and persecuted Muhammad. The prophet fled to another city, Medina, in A.D. 622. His flight, called the *Hegira*, is holy to Islam. Muslims date their calendar from this year. In Medina, Muhammad became a powerful leader. Before his death, the people living in Mecca became Muslims, too.

After Muhammad died, belief in Islam continued to spread. Its Arab followers (called *Moors* in North Africa and Spain) carved out an empire. They conquered Persia, Syria, and Egypt, and invaded Spain and France. However, internal struggles for power and European opposition helped to break up the Muslim empire after the 1200's.

Muslims believe that "There is no god but Allah [God], and Muhammad is the prophet of Allah." They believe in the same God Christians and Jews believe in, and in the religious teachers of the Old Testament, such as Abraham, Isaac, and Jacob. Muslims think of Jesus Christ as a great teacher, and believe that there will be a Judgment Day when the good will go to heaven and the wicked will go to hell.

Muslims pray five times each day, always facing toward Mecca. A *muezzin*, or crier, announces prayer time from the *minaret* (tower) attached to the *mosque*, or temple. An *imam*, or chief religious official, leads the people in prayer. Every able person must give *alms* (money) to the poor. During the holy month of *Ramadan*,

adult Muslims must *fast* (go without food or drink) between sunrise and sunset. Once during his lifetime, every Muslim is supposed to make a *hadj*, or visit, to the holy city of Mecca. Muslims are not supposed to drink liquor, eat pork, or gamble.

ALSO READ: BLACK MUSLIMS, KORAN, MOSQUE, MUHAMMAD.

ISLAND An island is a body of land entirely surrounded by water. In a way, even the continents are islands because they are surrounded by oceans. Australia is often called the "island-continent." But all the continents are very large, and the word "island" is most often used to mean a smaller body of land.

In the ocean, islands may be part of a continental shelf. These islands formed at the end of the last ice age, when the level of the ocean rose and covered low-lying areas at the edges of the continents. Newfoundland, off Canada's east coast, was formed this way. So were the British Isles. Many oceanic islands occur in groups called "island arcs," for example, the Aleutian Islands. These are volcanic islands and occur alongside deep trenches in the ocean floor, where one crustal plate (a rigid portion of the Earth's crust) is slipping beneath an-

▲ *Worshipers in an Islamic mosque. Most Muslims are Sunnis, followers of* sunna *(the way) of the prophet Muhammad. Shiite Muslims broke away from the main body of Muslims in the 600's. Today their main support is in Iran and Iraq.*

▼ *The island of Bora Bora in the Pacific Ocean is a fine example of an island formed by volcanoes. Near it are other islands made of coral.*

▲ *This tiny island is actually part of the Great Barrier Reef sticking out of the sea. It is off the northeast coast of Australia.*

▶ *Surtsey, an island off the coast of Iceland, was born in a flurry of steam and boiling sea in November 1963.*

The ten largest islands in the world are:

Greenland (N. Atlantic)
839,999 sq. mi.
2,175,429 sq. km

New Guinea (S. Pacific)
345,054 sq. mi.
893,621 sq. km

Borneo (Pacific)
289,859 sq. mi.
750,677 sq. km

Madagascar (Indian)
241,094 sq. mi.
624,385 sq. km

Baffin (North Atlantic)
183,810 sq. mi.
476,031 sq. km

Sumatra (Indian)
164,148 sq. mi.
425, 110 sq. km

Gt. Britain (N. Atlantic)
88,745 sq. mi.
229,831 sq. km

Honshu (North Pacific)
87,426 sq. mi.
226,416 sq. km

Ellesmere (Arctic)
82,119 sq. mi.
212,672 sq. km

Victoria (Arctic)
81,930 sq. mi.
212,182 sq. km

other. The friction caused by this movement heats the rocks until they erupt as volcanoes. Many small islands are simply large circular coral reefs called *atolls*.

Islands in rivers are sandbars or areas of hard rock that have resisted the action of the water that cut the riverbed.

Islands in lakes are usually higher parts of the lakebed exposed above the surface of the water.

ALSO READ: CONTINENT, CORAL, GREAT BARRIER REEF, MOUNTAIN, VOLCANO, PLATE TECTONICS.

ISOTOPE see ATOM.

ISRAEL Since the modern-day State of Israel was established in 1948, the Israeli people have changed a barren, nonproductive land into one of the most industrialized and advanced nations of the world. The Israelis have built modern towns, factories, and schools. A national irrigation project has made large parts of Israel, including the dry, rocky Negev Desert, a fertile land.

Israel is located in part of the area that was once Palestine. Ancient Israel was the traditional homeland of the Jewish people. It is also the birthplace of Christianity—the land where Jesus Christ lived. Jerusalem, the capital, is a holy city for the Muslims, as well as for Jews and Christians. (See the map with the article on the MIDDLE EAST.)

Israel is a narrow country, slightly larger than the state of New Jersey. The land in the north and east is hilly, but it is flat along the coast of the Mediterranean Sea. The Negev Desert in the southern part of the country occupies more than half of the total land area. The Jordan River Valley lies in the eastern part of the country. The lowest point of land in the world, the Dead Sea, is located there.

Israel has a warm climate throughout the year. Most of the rain falls in the winter. The northern part of the country receives more rain than the southern desert.

Israeli farmers grow much of their country's food. The principal crops include oranges and other citrus fruits, olives, barley, wheat, tomatoes, potatoes, figs, and corn. One type of farming community fre-

ISRAEL

Capital City: Jerusalem (460,000 people).
Area: 8,019 square miles (20,768 sq. km).
Population: 4,400,000.
Government: Republic.
Natural Resources: Potash, bromine and other salts, copper.
Export Products: Polished diamonds, machinery and other manufactures, chemicals, citrus fruits, processed foods.
Unit of Money: Shekel.
Official Languages: Hebrew, Arabic.

quently found in Israel is the *kibbutz*. People live and work together on a kibbutz, sharing the farm equipment and the money earned from the produce.

Large factories are located in and around Haifa and Tel Aviv. The principal industrial products are chemicals, electrical equipment, plastics, tires, metal goods, pharmaceuticals, processed foods, textiles, and polished diamonds.

In the 1800's, mass killings of Jews in Russia and other parts of Eastern Europe caused thousands of Jews to emigrate to Palestine. Great Britain received control of Palestine from the League of Nations after World War I (1918). The British and the League promised to make Palestine a "national homeland" for Jews. The Arabs living in Palestine and the surrounding countries were violently against having a Jewish nation there.

Nazi persecution in the 1930's forced thousands of Jews to flee from Germany and other European countries. Many settled in Palestine. Thousands more arrived after World War II. The Palestine Arabs began to attack the Jewish settlements. In order to stop the fighting, the British announced that only a small number of Jews could enter the country. This satisfied the Arabs, but the number of Jewish immigrants kept growing. Thousands of refugees waited on ships in the harbor at Haifa, hoping to be admitted.

The British government submitted the problem to the United Nations in 1947. The U.N. voted to divide Palestine into two separate states—one Arab and one Jewish. The British left Palestine in 1948, and the Jewish State of Israel was established. Many Palestinian Arabs left Israel to live in refugee camps.

Israel is a parliamentary democracy. The elected legislative body, the *Knesset*, elects the president and the prime minister. The nation has no written constitution, and authority lies with the legislature.

The tiny nation has had to defend its borders from its Arab neighbors since its birth. Border clashes, acts of sabotage, and a constant atmosphere of hostility have been the general state of affairs between Israel and the Arab

▼ *A group of Arabs plow the land and sow seed near the modern city of Bethlehem. The Church of the Nativity in that city is over a cave where, according to local tradition, Mary gave birth to Jesus.*

▲ *Thousands of Jewish settlers arrived at Haifa in Palestine (Israel) after World War II. In 1948, the State of Israel was created as a national homeland for the Jews.*

▼ *Nero, the emperor who ruled so badly that finally he had to flee from Rome. He was more interested in music and the arts than in ruling justly, and the Romans rose up against his cruelty.*

states since 1945. There have been bitter disputes over the land, the water supply, and the use of the Suez Canal.

In the Six-Day War of 1967, Israel captured territory from Egypt, Jordan, and Syria. Another war in 1973 between Israel and the Arabs ended in a U.N. ceasefire resolution. In 1979, Israel signed a peace treaty with Egypt. Relations with Egypt improved in the 1980's, but Israel clashed with other Arab countries. In 1982, Israel invaded southern Lebanon in order to destroy Arab PLO (Palestinian Liberation Organization) bases there. Israel's troops gradually withdrew in 1985.

ALSO READ: BEN-GURION, DAVID; DEAD SEA; EGYPT; ISLAM; JERUSALEM; JEWISH HISTORY; JORDAN; JUDAISM; MIDDLE EAST; PALESTINE.

ITALIAN see ROMANCE LANGUAGES.

ITALIAN HISTORY The Italian peninsula in Europe has a history of almost ceaseless warfare within its shores and countless invasions from abroad. For most of its history, Italy was not united as one nation.

About 1,000 years before the birth of Jesus Christ, many different tribes lived in the Italian peninsula. The most powerful people were the Etruscans. Their homeland was a region in central Italy. They conquered lands to the north and south but were never able to take over the whole peninsula.

The Italian city of Rome succeeded where the Etruscans had failed. The Roman people not only conquered the whole of Italy, but by 27 B.C., they had also created a huge empire in Europe and the Middle East. The Roman Empire prospered for about 500 years. But in the A.D. 300's, German tribes from the north began to invade the western part of the empire. The last Roman emperor of the West, Romulus Augustulus, was defeated by a German barbarian, Odoacer, in A.D. 476. From that date until the mid-1800's, Italy was for the most part divided into a group of small states. These states fought continually among themselves. They found it difficult to combine, even against a foreign invader. Italy was overrun again and again by more powerful peoples from other parts of Europe.

From about A.D. 60, Rome had been the headquarters of the pope, leader of the Roman Catholic church. In A.D. 572, Italy was invaded by a fierce German tribe, the Lombards, who conquered many regions and threatened to attack Rome. The pope appealed for help to the most powerful ruler in Europe, the king of the Franks. Later, the Frankish king, Charlemagne, finally drove the Lombards out of Italy. He was crowned Emperor of the Romans in A.D. 800 by Pope Leo III. The Franks gave the pope a large area of land in central Italy. This area became known as the Papal States. The popes soon became strong enough to resist attempts by invaders to take over the Papal States.

After the death of Charlemagne, the Franks and the Germans struggled for control of Italy. In A.D. 962, northern Italy was captured by a powerful German king, Otto the Great. Otto was crowned Holy Roman Emperor by the pope. For the next 500 years, Italy was dominated by the Holy Roman emperors and the popes. By this time, many Italian cities had become important trading centers. They grew wealthy and powerful, and some became self-governing states. Among the greatest of these city-states were Florence, Genoa, Milan, Pisa, and Venice. Genoa and Venice were ruled by powerful magistrates, called *doges,* who were similar to today's mayors. Wealthy merchants in the cities encouraged the work of artists and scholars. The Italian cities became the birthplace of the great movement of new ideas known as the Renaissance.

Italy was invaded by France in 1494. Shortly afterward, the Holy Roman Empire was split between Spain and Austria. For the next 400 years, Italy became the battleground for struggles among these three powers. At one point, northern Italy was united as the Kingdom of Italy by the French emperor Napoleon I. But after Napoleon was defeated at the Battle of Waterloo in 1815, Italy was once again divided among several rulers.

By the mid-1800's, the Italian people began to speak of fighting for a free and united Italy. Several revolutions were organized against the Austrians, who ruled Italy at that time.

▼ *Lorenzo dei Medici was one of a family of powerful Italian rulers during the Renaissance. A virtual dictator, he was also a great patron of the arts and sciences.*

By 1860, Count Cavour, the prime minister of the Kingdom of Sardinia, had united most of northern Italy against Austria. The same year, the Italian patriot, Giuseppe Garibaldi, led his army of "red shirts" to victory in southern Italy. By 1870, the whole peninsula had been united as the Kingdom of Italy. The first king was Victor Emmanuel II of Sardinia.

The long years of war had left the Italian people poor and hungry. The people became dissatisfied with the new government when it did very little to help them. Italy's rulers were more interested in gaining power and influence abroad. During World War I (1914–1918), Italy fought with Great Britain and France against Austria-Hungary and Germany. The Italian people became even poorer, and when a new leader, Benito Mussolini, promised to bring back the wealth and glory of the Roman Empire, many people—including King Victor Emmanuel III—supported him. Mussolini became premier of Italy in 1922. He organized a fascist government with himself as dictator. In 1936, he signed a treaty with the German dictator, Adolf Hitler. Italy, Japan, and Germany were defeated by Great Britain and her allies in World War II (1939–1945), and Mussolini was killed.

In 1946, free elections were held in Italy. The people voted to end the monarchy, and Italy became a republic. The government began programs to improve the lives of the Italian people. Northern Italy is now one of the most industrialized regions of Europe. But the Italian people are still split by fierce struggles between different political parties. The Communist party in Italy has become one of the largest Communist parties outside of the Soviet Union and China.

ALSO READ: CHARLEMAGNE; DANTE ALIGHIERI; DICTATOR; ETRUSCAN; FASCISM; HOLY ROMAN EMPIRE; ITALY; MUSSOLINI, BENITO; NAPOLEON

▲ *An old print of the Arsenal in Venice, where its ships were built. Trade by sea with Muslim countries brought Venice immense wealth.*

▲ *King Victor Emmanuel III* (left) *riding with Benito Mussolini* (center). *The king allowed Mussolini to become dictator of Italy.*

Italy is the world's largest producer of wine, with nearly 8 billion liters a year out of a world production of 35 billion bottles. Italians drink more wine than the people of any other nation do—over 90 liters (24 gallons) in a year per each person in the population.

BONAPARTE; POPE; RENAISSANCE; ROME; ROME, ANCIENT; VENICE; WORLD WAR I; WORLD WAR II.

ITALY Visitors like Italy for its scenic landscapes, ancient ruins, beautiful architecture, and great art museums. Tourism is an important business in this usually sunny country, well known also for its lovely beaches, lake resorts, and Alpine ski lodges.

The 700-mile (1,125-km) long Italian peninsula, shaped like a boot, extends into the Mediterranean Sea. The snowcapped Alps Mountains rise along its northern border, which is shared with France, Switzerland, and Austria. A chain of mountains, the Apennines, runs down the center of Italy. The mountains often rise from the very edge of the sea. Many of Italy's coastal towns are crowded into

narrow spaces between cliffs and the sea. Italy's major valley lies just south of the Alps, where the Po River cuts through the land. The Mediterranean islands of Sicily, Sardinia, Lipari, Pantellerina, Elba, Capri, and Ischia are also part of Italy.

Rome is the capital of Italy. It is also the world capital of the Roman Catholic Church. The pope rules over Vatican City, a tiny independent church state located in the heart of Rome.

Before World War II, most Italians were farmers. After the war, many factories were built and Italy became an important industrial nation and a member of the European Common Market. The most important farming and industrial area is the Po Valley. Textiles, chemicals, machinery, and automobiles are produced in factories in the valley's cities. Cattle and sheep graze in the lush pastures, and orchards produce peaches and apples. In parts of western and southern Italy, farmers grow oranges, lemons, and olives. Grapes for wine are cultivated throughout the country. Italy is one of the leading wine-producing countries in the world.

In southern Italy, the soil is poor and farming is difficult. Most rivers dry out during the hot summers. Farmers work very hard to earn a living. They often plant their crops on steep hillsides where the soil is held in place by stone walls. Most Italian farm families live in small towns.

Before 1870, Italians were not ruled by one national government. The region was a patchwork of small kingdoms, independent territories, and Papal States (areas governed by the pope, or Roman Catholic Church). When the country was finally united it was ruled by a king. Benito Mussolini, a fascist dictator, became the country's leader in 1922, although the king still reigned. Italy became a republic after World War II. A president, prime minister, cabinet, and parliament form the govern-

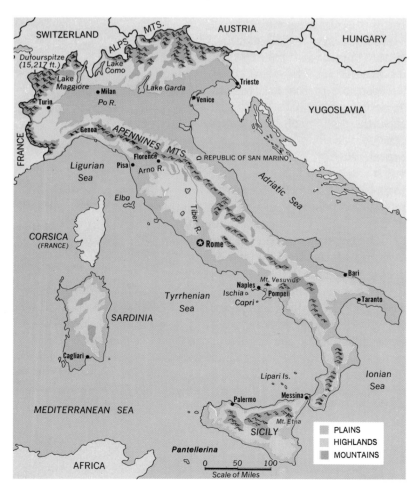

ITALY

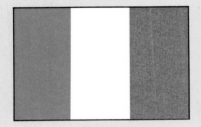

Capital City: Rome (2,831,000 people).
Area: 116,314 square miles (301,230 sq. km).
Population: 57,400,000.
Government: Republic.
Natural Resources: Some oil and natural gas, mercury, sulfur.
Export Products: Machinery, vehicles, iron and steel, textiles, fruit and vegetables, wine.
Unit of Money: Lira.
Official Language: Italian.

ment today. Italy has had many governments since World War II. Few have lasted much more than a year. Labor strikes and student protests have unsettled the country. In the 1970's and 1980's, atrocities committed by the Red Brigades, a small group of extreme leftists, and Palestinian terrorists created fear in the country.

ALSO READ: ADRIATIC SEA; FASCISM; FLORENCE; ITALIAN HISTORY; MEDITERRANEAN SEA; MUSSOLINI, BENITO; ROME; ROME, ANCIENT; VATICAN CITY.

▼ *In Italy you are never far from the sea. This small fishing village is located on the western coast near the city of La Spezia.*

IVORY COAST (Côte d'Ivoire)
When European explorers first visited West Africa, they set up trading posts for ivory in a particularly fertile region of the coast. This region became known as the Ivory Coast. Today, the country located there is an independent republic about the size of the state of New Mexico. It is on the southern coast of the West African bulge, on the Gulf of Guinea. The Mali Republic and Burkina Faso lie to the north. Guinea and Liberia are its western neighbors, and Ghana lies to the east. (See the map with the article on AFRICA.)

In the Ivory Coast, thick rain forests spread inland from the coastal

▼ *The Leaning Tower of Pisa, one of Italy's best-known monuments, was completed in 1350. It leans because the ground underneath it began to sink soon after the first three stories were built.*

IVORY COAST

The Ivory Coast produces twice as much cocoa as any other country in Africa. It is also the largest producer of coffee.

capital, Abidjan. Farther north, grassy plains, called *savannas*, rise to an area of rolling hills and mountains. The climate is hot and humid in the coastal region and cooler in the north.

The people of the Ivory Coast are called Ivorians. The official language is French, but most people speak one of the more than 60 local African languages. About two-thirds of the people follow African tribal religions. A smaller number are Muslims or Christians.

The Ivory Coast has long been one of the most prosperous West African nations. Numerous crops thrive on the fertile soil. Bananas, pineapples, coffee, cocoa, cotton, and palm oil are important products. Rubber and timber (mahogany and other hardwoods) are also valuable sources of income.

There are deposits of diamonds, manganese, and other minerals in the ground. Rich fisheries exist along the coast. Among the country's main industries are food and lumber processing, oil refining, assembly of automobiles, textiles, and shipbuilding.

The first Europeans to visit the region of the Ivory Coast were Portugese explorers in the 1400's. French missionaries and traders arrived in the 1600's. The French claimed the region as a colony of France in 1893. The Ivory Coast gained its independence in 1960. It is governed by a president and his cabinet of ministers. A national assembly is elected by the people.

ALSO READ: AFRICA.

IVORY COAST (CÔTE d'IVOIRE)

Capital City: Abidjan (1,800,000 people).
Area: 124,504 square miles (322,440 sq. km).
Population: 11,800,000.
Government: One-party republic.
Natural Resources: Oil, diamonds, lumber.
Export Products: Cocoa, coffee, lumber, oil products.
Unit of Money: Franc of the African Financial Community.
Official Language: French.

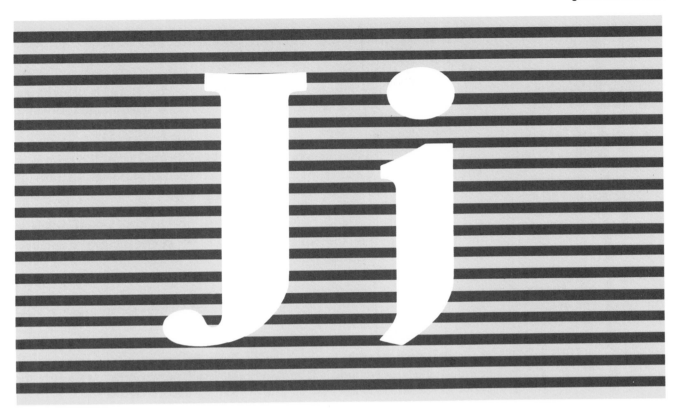

JACKAL The jackal is a large-eared wild dog. It is generally light brownish yellow or tawny in color, with the tip of its bushy tail always dark. A fully grown jackal is more than 2 feet (60 cm) long and weighs about 20 pounds (10 kg). It resembles a small wolf or coyote. Jackals are found in Asia, Africa, and parts of Europe. They are usually seen in pairs, but often hunt in packs of 5 to 20.

Jackals are mainly scavengers that feed on the remains of dead animals. But they also hunt small animals, such as poultry and baby antelopes. Their hunting is usually done at night, when their yapping and howling can be heard. Jackals also eat fruits and vegetables. During the day, they hide in burrows, caves, tall grass, or bushes. Sometimes jackals interbreed with domestic dogs and wolves.

The *golden*, or *Asiatic, jackal* ranges from central Asia to North Africa. Golden jackals usually hunt in packs. The *side-striped jackal* and *black-backed jackal* live in eastern and southern Africa and are mostly solitary animals. The side-striped jackal has a pair of light and dark stripes on each side of its body. The black-backed jackal is highly valued for its rich, attractive fur.

ALSO READ: COYOTE, DOG, WOLF.

JACKRABBIT see RABBITS AND HARES.

▼ *The jackal, a wild dog, resembles a wolf but is smaller and more slightly built.*

Andrew Jackson had a fiery temper that caused him to be involved in several duels. In 1806, he fought a lawyer named Charles Dickinson, and Dickinson was killed. Jackson received a serious wound.

During Andrew Jackson's term of office the first American steam locomotive was built and used for passenger service. Jackson was the first President to ride in a train.

JACKSON, ANDREW (1767–1845) Jackson's admirers called him "The People's President." The six men who were Presidents before him had been well-to-do, educated men from Virginia and Massachusetts. Jackson, however, came from a poor South Carolina frontier family. He was born a few days after his father died. Young Andy had little schooling, but he had much courage. He was 13 when British soldiers invaded the Carolinas during the American Revolution. He joined the American volunteers. Later, Andy and his brother Robert were captured by the British. A British officer ordered Andy to clean his boots, but the boy refused. The officer cut Andy's head and hand with a sword. Robert also refused and was wounded. The two boys were marched 40 miles (65 km) to a prison, where they both soon caught smallpox. Andy got better, but Robert died. Their mother later died of a fever she had caught while caring for the wounded. Andy's only other brother had been killed earlier in the war. At the age of 14, he was left without a family.

He stayed with relatives and tried various jobs, including saddle-making and teaching school. He finally turned to studying law and became a lawyer at the age of 20. In 1788, he was appointed attorney general for the area that was soon to become Tennessee, and he moved to Nashville. There, he met and married Rachel Robards. At the time of the marriage, Mrs. Robards thought that her previous husband had divorced her. But the divorce did not go through until she had been married to Jackson for two years. The two were remarried. But Jackson's enemies often criticized his wife. Mrs. Jackson was hurt by the attacks and avoided public life. Jackson served briefly in the U.S. House of Representatives and the Senate but returned home to Tennessee in 1798 to become a judge.

Jackson became a military hero during the War of 1812 against the British. His soldiers called him "Old Hickory" because he was so tough. He led the Americans to victory at the Battle of New Orleans. The battle was fought after the peace treaty had been signed, but word of this had not yet reached New Orleans. Jackson became a national hero.

In 1818, Jackson led a raid on the Seminole Indians in Florida, which was still owned by Spain. He became the first governor of Florida after Spain sold it to the United States in 1821 but resigned after four months.

Jackson ran for President in 1824. He received more electoral votes than the other candidates, but he did not

ANDREW JACKSON
SEVENTH PRESIDENT   MARCH 4, 1829–MARCH 4, 1837

Born: March 15, 1767, Waxhaw, South Carolina
Parents: Andrew and Elizabeth Hutchinson Jackson
Education: Mostly self-educated
Religion: Presbyterian
Occupation: Lawyer and army officer
Political Party: Democratic (formerly the Democratic-Republican Party)
State Represented: Tennessee
Married: 1791 to Rachel Donelson Robards (1767–1828)
Children: 1 adopted son
Died: June 8, 1845, The Hermitage, Nashville, Tennessee
Buried: The Hermitage, Nashville, Tennessee

have the necessary majority. The election was decided by the U.S. House of Representatives, according to the election rules of the Constitution. They decided that John Quincy Adams should be President. Jackson ran again in 1828. This time he won the necessary majority and was elected President. After the inauguration, Jackson invited the crowd into the White House. In their haste to shake hands with their hero, the people overturned chairs and tables, broke dishes, and tore curtains. Jackson escaped through a window.

Jackson gave many government jobs to his political associates. This was called the "spoils system." Under this sytem, the winner in an election gives jobs to friends and can fire the people who previously held these jobs.

In 1832, Congress passed a bill to renew the charter of the Bank of the United States. This bank, in which government funds were deposited, was controlled by private individuals. The bank was accused of favoring rich people. Jackson vetoed (refused to sign) the bill. He said he was opposed "to the advancement of the few at the expense of the many." He was reelected President that year.

Jackson also took a firm stand when the South Carolina legislature voted to *nullify* (reject) an import tax law that Congress had passed. The President threatened to use force, if necessary, to make sure the law was obeyed. He believed that the Union would be in danger if one state was permitted to nullify a law passed by the Federal Government. He said in his last address as President, "By every sacrifice, this Union must be preserved."

After the Presidency, Jackson returned to Tennessee. He lived at the Hermitage—a handsome house he had built near Nashville.

ALSO READ: ADAMS, JOHN QUINCY; CALHOUN, JOHN C.; CLAY, HENRY; WAR OF 1812.

JACKSON, HELEN HUNT
(1830–1885) The American writer, Helen Hunt Jackson, became well known for her work to help the American Indians.

Born in Amherst, Massachusetts, she was a lifelong friend of the poet, Emily Dickinson. In 1852, Helen Maria Fiske (her maiden name) married Major E. B. Hunt, who was accidentally killed 11 years later. She began writing poetry for magazines, using the signature "H. H.," which soon became her pseudonym (pen name). In 1875, she married William S. Jackson and moved to Colorado Springs, Colorado. She also wrote children's stories, novels, and travel sketches.

Since childhood, Helen Hunt Jackson had been interested in the American Indians. Her book, *A Century of Dishonor*, published in 1881, was a historical account of the U.S. government's mistreatment of the Indians. Mrs. Jackson was made a special investigator to look into the condition of the Mission Indians of California.

Ramona, her romantic novel about Indian life, appeared in 1884. The story's heroine, Ramona, saw the Indians being driven to extinction by "civilization." Helen Hunt Jackson won much fame with this book, which was made into a motion picture three times.

ALSO READ: INDIANS, AMERICAN.

JACKSON, MAHALIA (1911–1972)
One of America's most famous gospel and concert singers was Mahalia Jackson, the granddaughter of slaves. She was also a recording artist and a devoted civil rights worker.

She was born in New Orleans, Louisiana, where she sang in the choir of the Baptist church. Young Mahalia also listened to the music of the street singers and soon developed her own style of gospel singing.

▲ *Helen Hunt Jackson, writer and champion of the cause of the American Indian.*

▲ *Mahalia Jackson, American gospel singer.*

▲ *A jai alai player turns and scoops the ball with his basketlike cesta.*

▲ *Stonewall Jackson, Confederate general.*

At the age of 15, Mahalia moved to Chicago, where her singing in churches and revival meetings attracted much attention. She sang on radio and television and made many recordings. In 1950, she sang in Carnegie Hall, New York. Her strong contralto voice and the deep religious feeling she brought to her songs won her many admirers.

Mahalia toured abroad, gaining new admirers in many countries. She appeared at American jazz festivals, such as the Newport Jazz Festival. She sang *Negro spirituals*—religious folk songs handed down from generation to generation—as well as *gospel songs*—religious songs written by composers. In 1963, Mahalia Jackson sang for the people who marched in Washington, D.C., to demand equal rights for America's black citizens. She also sang at the funeral of the great civil rights leader, Martin Luther King, in 1968.

JACKSON, THOMAS JONATHAN ("STONEWALL") (1824–1863) Stonewall Jackson was one of the most famous Confederate Army generals during the Civil War. He was born in Clarksburg, Virginia (now West Virginia). He graduated from the U.S. Military Academy, served in the Mexican War, and taught at the Virginia Military Institute for ten years.

When the Civil War began, he joined the Confederate Army. He fought in the first Battle of Bull Run at Manassas, Virginia, in July 1861. A Confederate officer said that Jackson and his soldiers stood "like a stone wall" against the Union Army. The South won the battle, and Jackson became known as "Stonewall."

Serving under General Robert E. Lee, Jackson and his troops were victorious in the Shenandoah Valley, at Fredericksburg, and at the second Battle of Bull Run. Jackson became famous for the speed with which his

soldiers could march from place to place. He was greatly respected by them and his fellow officers.

In May 1863, Jackson's army helped defeat a Northern army at Chancellorsville, Virginia. But as Jackson returned from the front lines on horseback at twilight, Southern troops thought he was an enemy officer and shot him. His last words were, "Let us cross the river and rest in the shade."

ALSO READ: CIVIL WAR.

JAGUAR see CAT, WILD.

JAI ALAI The fast, dangerous game of jai alai began in the Basque region of northern Spain in the 1600's. Today, it is a popular sport in the United States, Latin America, the Philippine Islands, and Europe. In jai alai, spectators often bet on games.

The sport is played on an indoor court, called a *cancha*, located in an arena, called a *fronton*. The court is about 176 feet (54 m) long and 55 feet (17 m) wide, bounded on the front, back, and one side by 44-foot (13.4-m) high walls. The audience sits behind netted wire on the fourth side.

The game is similar to handball, except that the players use basketlike *cestas*. The cesta is made of a wooden frame and light, tough reeds, woven together to form a curved scoop. The cesta, attached to the player's forearm, permits the player to catch the ball and throw it against the wall at high speed.

The jai alai ball, called a *pelota*, is slightly smaller than a baseball. In a jai alai game, the ball sometimes reaches a speed of 150 miles an hour (240 km/hr). The ball is made of a special, very hard rubber and is covered with goatskin.

The object of the game is to throw the ball against the walls in such a way that it cannot be returned. Depending on the number of players, 6 to 30 points are needed to win a game.

ALSO READ: HANDBALL.

JAMAICA see WEST INDIES.

JAMES, JESSE see OUTLAW.

JAMES, KINGS OF ENGLAND

James was the name of two kings of England.

James (1566–1625) was the son of Mary, Queen of Scots, and a cousin of Queen Elizabeth I of England. When he was one year old, his mother was forced to give up the throne of Scotland, and he became King James VI of Scotland. When Queen Elizabeth died without any children in 1603, James VI was also crowned King James I of England. In this way, England and Scotland were joined under one ruler.

James believed that God, and not the people, gave the kings the right to rule. This belief, known as the "divine right of kings," made him very unpopular with the English people. While James I was king, the first permanent English settlement in America, Jamestown, was founded (1607) and named after him. James I is also remembered for the poetic English translation of the Bible, the King James Version.

James II (1633–1701) was the grandson of James I. His father, King Charles I, was beheaded after being defeated in the English Civil War. When James became king, he organized the British expedition that seized the Dutch colony of New Amsterdam in America. In his honor, the colony was renamed New York, because he had been the Duke of York and Albany before becoming king. Fort Orange on the Hudson River became Fort Albany.

James II became king of England and Scotland in 1685, after the death of his older brother, Charles II. James II believed in the divine right of kings, just as his grandfather and father had. James was a devout Roman Catholic, and most of the English people were Protestants. James tried to force them to become Catholic like himself. He persecuted and imprisoned those who refused. The English Protestants finally asked William, Prince of Orange, to lead a rebellion against the king. William was a Dutch prince who had married James's daughter, Mary. William landed in England with an army in November 1688. James II fled to France without fighting. William and Mary were then crowned king and queen.

ALSO READ: CHARLES, KINGS OF ENGLAND; MARY, QUEEN OF SCOTS; WILLIAM AND MARY.

JAMESTOWN The first permanent English settlement in America was Jamestown, Virginia, founded in 1607.

In late December, 1606, a group of English merchants, called the London Company, sent colonists to the New World aboard three ships, *Discovery, Susan Constant*, and *Godspeed*. The colonists landed on a small peninsula on the present-day James River on May 14, 1607. There they built a fort to protect themselves against Indian attacks. The new community was called "King James His Towne" in honor of the English king, James I. Later, the name was shortened to Jamestown.

The area chosen for the new colony was low and marshy. Many of the colonists became ill. All would have starved, but their leader, Captain John Smith, got the neighboring Indians to sell them food. He also made the colonists work to grow some of the needed food. The winter of 1609–1610 was called the "starving time." Many of the colonists died from hunger and disease.

Lord De La Warr, the new gover-

▲ *James VI of Scotland became James I of England.*

▲ *James II of England.*

Some people believe that the Jamestown colony was saved when Pocahontas, daughter of the mighty Indian chief Powhatan, stopped the killing of John Smith by the Indians. Pocahontas was later converted to Christianity and married John Rolfe, one of the colonial leaders.

▲ *An early illustration of events in the Jamestown colony shows Captain John Smith taking an Indian chief as his prisoner. Smith explored the rivers of Virginia and mapped the area.*

nor, arrived after that disastrous winter ended. He encouraged the remaining colonists to stay, and the town began to prosper. The colonists began raising hogs and growing Indian corn and tobacco, which soon became the colony's most important product.

The first legislative assembly in America met in Jamestown in 1619. Jamestown was the capital of the new colony of Virginia, until the capital was moved to Williamsburg in 1699.

Today, part of Jamestown lies within the Colonial National Historical Park. Exact copies of the fort and other early buildings have been built. Visitors can tour the buildings and watch people performing crafts and chores the way the early colonists did them. Anchored offshore are models of the ships that brought the colonists to the New World.

ALSO READ: POCAHONTAS; POWHATAN; SMITH, CAPTAIN JOHN; VIRGINIA.

JAMS AND JELLIES Most foods stay fresh for a short time. Then bacteria, yeasts, and molds from the air cause them to spoil. The more water and the less sugar a food contains, the more quickly it spoils. Many fruits contain 75 percent water and 10 to 15 percent sugar. They can be preserved (kept from spoiling) by reducing the water in them and adding sugar. In this form they become jams and jellies. Many people like to make jams and jellies at home. But in the United States

most are now made in factories.

Jelly is made by boiling fruit and water together until the fruit is soft. A special jelly bag, or a cheesecloth bag, is then placed over a bowl. The mixture is poured or pressed through the bag into the bowl below. The collected juice is measured, and a certain amount is put into a pot on the stove. Sugar is added. *Pectin*, a natural fruit substance, may also be added to thicken the mixture. Some fruits, such as apples, currants, grapes, and blackberries, contain large amounts of pectin. They may not need additional pectin when made into jelly.

The mixture is boiled and stirred until it reaches *setting point* and starts to thicken. The pot is then removed from the stove, and the mixture is skimmed to remove the white foam that has collected on top. The jelly is poured into clean jars. Each jar is sealed with a special cap, or with a layer of wax. The lid is put on after the wax hardens.

Jam is made in the same way, except that whole or crushed fruit—not just their juice—is used.

■ LEARN BY DOING

You can make some apple jelly at home, but make sure you have the help of an adult. Cut several pounds of apples into quarters and place in a saucepan. Add water until you can just see it through the top layer of fruit. Cook, uncovered, until the fruit is soft, then strain the mixture through a jelly bag. Measure the strained juice into a

Add water to chopped apples

Boil the mixture

Ladle into sterile jars

large pan. Add ¾ to 1 cup of sugar to each cup of juice. Boil the mixture for about 10 minutes then test to see if it is beginning to set by putting a teaspoon of the mixture in a saucer well chilled in the refrigerator. If the jelly wrinkles when you push it with a spoon, it is ready. Pour the mixture into sterile jars and seal with melted paraffin. ■

JANUARY January is named for the Roman god, Janus. He was a god with two faces—one face looking forward and one looking backward. He was the god of doors and gates, and also the god of beginnings.

January did not always begin the year. In ancient Rome it was probably the eleventh month. Julius Caesar ordered the calendar to be changed. As a result of those changes, January became the first month of the year and was named after Janus.

January's special flower is the carnation or the snowdrop, and the garnet is its birthstone. January occurs in winter in the Northern Hemisphere (north of the equator), but in the Southern Hemisphere, January is a summer month. The first day of January is New Year's Day, and on that day many people make New Year's resolutions. January sixth, 12 days after Christmas, is the feast of Epiphany, the day the Three Wise Men came to visit the infant Jesus. It is the last day of the Christmas season. The evening before Epiphany is called Twelfth Night. Twelfth Night, rather than Christmas, is the time for gift-giving in Mexico and some other countries. An old legend warns that if you do not take down your Christmas decorations by Twelfth Night, elves will get in and mess up your house.

ALSO READ: CALENDAR, MONTH.

January's flower, the carnation

DATES OF SPECIAL EVENTS IN JANUARY

1 • New Year's Day.
• Paul Revere was born (1735).
• First United States federal income tax (1862).
• Abraham Lincoln issued the Emancipation Proclamation, freeing the slaves in the Confederate states (1863).
• The Commonwealth of Australia was formed (1901).
• Fidel Castro became leader of Cuba (1959).
5 • Nellie Tayloe Ross became first woman governor of a state, Wyoming (1925).
6 • Joan of Arc was born (1412).
7 • First United States Presidential election was held (1789).
• Transatlantic telephone service between London and New York began (1927).
• President Millard Fillmore was born (1800).
8 • The Eleventh Amendment to the U.S. Constitution was adopted, restricting powers of U.S. Supreme Court (1798).
• U.S. troops under Andrew Jackson defeated the British at the Battle of New Orleans (1815).
9 • President Richard M. Nixon was born (1913).
10 • First subway system in the world opened in London (1863).
• The first great oil strike occurred in Texas (1901).
• The League of Nations was established (1920).
• First United Nations General Assembly meeting, in London (1946).
11 • Alexander Hamilton, American statesman, was born (1755).
• Sir John A. Macdonald, first prime minister of Canada after confederation, was born (1815).
12 • John Hancock, first signer of the Declaration of Independence, was born (1737).
• Jack London, American writer, was born (1876).
14 • Albert Schweitzer, jungle missionary and philosopher, was born (1875).
15 • Martin Luther King, Jr., American civil rights leader, was born (1929).
17 • Wassailing the apple tree, an old custom, takes place every year in Carhampton, England. Villagers gather around the largest tree and sing, "Old apple tree, old apple tree, we've come to wassail thee." The custom was originally carried out in the hope of a good apple crop.
• Benjamin Franklin, American statesman, was born (1706).
18 • Daniel Webster, American statesman, was born (1782).
19 • Robert E. Lee, Commander in Chief of the Confederate Armies, was born (1807).
• Edgar Allan Poe, American author, was born (1809).
20 • Inauguration Day for U.S. Presidents (every four years). Established 1937.
21 • *Nautilus,* first atomic submarine, was launched (1954).
22 • Lord Byron, English poet, was born (1788).
24 • Gold was first discovered in California (1848).
25 • Robert Burns, Scottish poet, was born (1759).
• Transcontinental telephone service began in U.S. (1915).
26 • President William McKinley was born (1843).
27 • Lewis Carroll, author of *Alice in Wonderland,* was born (1832).
• United States Coast Guard was established (1915).
29 • First successful gasoline-powered car was patented by Carl Friedrich Benz (1886).
• American League in professional baseball was formed (1900).
30 • President Franklin D. Roosevelt was born (1882).
• Adolf Hitler was named chancellor (head) of Germany (1933).
• Mahatma Gandhi, Indian political leader, was assassinated (1948).

▲ *The samurai warrior was the Japanese version of the medieval knight. This suit of samurai armor was designed both to protect its owner in battle and impress his enemies with its splendor.*

There is an average of four earthquake shocks a day in some parts of Japan.

JAPAN Japan, the "land of the rising sun," is smaller in size than the state of California, but it is the third-ranking industrial power of the world. This Asian nation is made up of four large islands—Hokkaido, Honshu, Shikoku, and Kyushu—and more than 3,000 smaller islands. Tokyo, the capital and largest city, is located on the largest of the islands, Honshu.

Land and Climate Japan is covered with mountains. Many of them are volcanoes. The most famous mountain, Fujiyama (Mt. Fuji), is topped by snow most of the year. The country also has many lakes, waterfalls, and rivers.

The climate of Japan varies greatly from one end of the island chain to the other. Kyushu, the southernmost island, has a subtropical climate like that of northern Florida. Hokkaido, in the North, has cool summers and snowy winters. The islands receive plenty of rain. Sometimes hurricanes, called *typhoons*, sweep over Japan from the Pacific.

Less than one-fifth of the land in Japan is suitable for farming. But the Japanese have learned to cultivate carefully the soil that can be farmed, so that their crop yields are among the highest in the world. They have built special terraces on hillsides for growing rice and tea. Soybeans, cereal grains, and fruits are also grown. Japanese farms produce about 70 percent of the country's food.

The waters around Japan are rich with fish, which is also an important food of the Japanese. Salmon, tuna, lobsters, and crabs are major catches. Japan ranks as one of the world's leading fishing countries. Its fishing fleet sails all over the world. Japanese ships search the Arctic and Antarctic for whales. Japan exports much frozen, dried, and canned fish.

People Most Japanese belong to the Buddhist or Shinto religions. Shinto is an ancient religion of Japan in which the spirits of nature and of ancestors are worshiped. Some Japanese today are Christians.

The Japanese had no system of writing their language before the A.D. 700's. Then they learned to use a form of writing similar to the Chinese. *Characters*, or small line drawings, are used to represent entire words or ideas. Today, nearly all Japanese can read as well as write.

The Japanese appreciate beauty in everything around them. This love of beauty has produced some of the world's greatest works of art. Japanese artists and craftworkers excel in wood carving, flower arranging, delicate paintings, and architecture.

History Marco Polo, the Venetian who went to China, heard about

JAPAN

Capital City: Tokyo (8,390,000 people).
Area: 143,751 square miles (372,286 sq. km).
Population: 123,000,000.
Government: Monarchy.
Natural Resources: Some coal and various metals.
Export Products: Machinery and transport equipment, electronic goods, chemicals, textiles.
Unit of Money: Yen.
Official Language: Japanese.

Cipangu (Japan) and wrote about it in his travel diaries in 1229. The first Europeans to go to Japan were Portugese sailors in 1543. Six years later the Roman Catholic missionary, Saint Francis Xavier, arrived and began to teach Christianity. At first, missionaries were welcomed, and some Japanese became Christians. After some years, the rulers became afraid that the Europeans might send soldiers to conquer Japan. In 1637, they killed many Christians and closed the country to all foreigners except the Dutch (who had sent no missionaries). Japan was isolated from the rest of the world for more than 200 years.

In 1853, Commodore Matthew Perry was sent to Japan to establish diplomatic and trade relations. He persuaded the Japanese to open two ports for American trade. Soon other nations began to trade with Japan. The Japanese learned much from these countries and developed industries and military forces. Japan became one of the world's great powers by the end of World War I. During the next 20 years, the Japanese expanded their empire by conquest. In 1941 the Japanese carried out a sur-

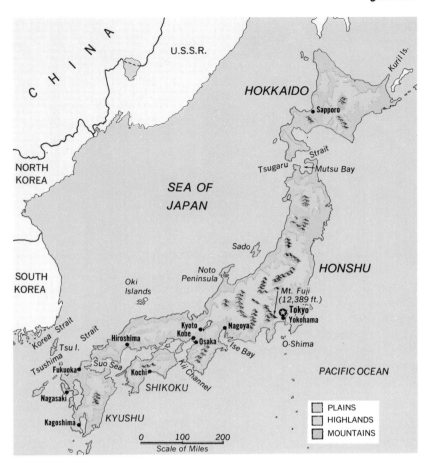

prise bombing attack on the U.S. Navy fleet at Pearl Harbor, Honolulu, bringing the United States into World War II. Japan had to give up all its occupied territories after its defeat by the United States in 1945.

Since World War II, Japan has become a great industrial power, in spite of having very few mineral resources. It is one of the world's top steel producers, yet the iron ore and

▼ *Japan is a chain of volcanic islands. Forests cover the country's mountain slopes and hills. Fish is a major food, and only about 15 percent of the land is farmed.*

▲ *Japan is one of the world's chief producers of electronic equipment. In this Japanese factory, television sets are checked as they move along a conveyor belt.*

According to tradition, the Japanese throne has been occupied by the members of the same family since the 600's B.C. The present emperor is the 125th in succession.

Japan is a small, crowded country and land is very expensive. The average cost of a piece of land for a house is 20 times what it would cost in the United States.

most of the coal needed to make steel are brought from other countries. Almost all its oil comes from the Middle East. The Japanese are highly skilled in technical fields. Japan is the largest shipbuilder and the largest automobile manufacturer in the world. The Japanese electronics industry is important, too. The country exports millions of television sets, radios, cameras, and other electrical products all over the world.

Japan was ruled by emperors for thousands of years. The emperors were believed to be descended from the sun god and had absolute power. After World War II, the emperor was forced to give up most of his power. Japan today is a constitutional monarchy, with an emperor who has no real power, and a democratic form of government.

ALSO READ: ASIA; PERRY, OLIVER HAZARD AND MATTHEW; WORLD WAR II.

JASON In the myths of ancient Greece, one of the bravest men was Jason. He was the son of Aeson, king of Iolcus, whose throne had been stolen by Pelias, Jason's uncle. Pelias promised Jason the throne if he would bring him the marvelous Golden Fleece—golden wool cut from a magic ram. Jason sailed off in a ship named the *Argo*, accompanied

▲ *This scene painted on an ancient Greek vase shows Jason attacking a monster.*

by the bravest men he could find. He and his crew were called the *Argonauts*. They survived several dangerous adventures during their trip, including an encounter with monsters called Harpies, who were half human and half bird. But at last the Argonauts reached Colchis, where the king forced Jason to fight two fire-breathing dragons and a bull. Medea, the king's daughter, helped Jason destroy the monsters and capture the fleece. Jason left Colchis with Medea, whom he later married. Some years later, however, Jason tired of her, and went off to marry the princess of Corinth. In revenge, Medea murdered the princess and her own children. For many years, Jason wandered until, as an old man, he was killed when the prow of the *Argo* fell on him.

ALSO READ: GREEK LITERATURE, MYTHOLOGY.

JAVA see INDONESIA.

JAZZ The most truly American music, jazz began in the early 1900's as a form of folk music created by poor black people, rather than by professional musicians. Since then it has gained worldwide popularity and is played in nightclubs and concert halls.

Early History Following the Civil War, many blacks came to New Orleans, Louisiana. With them they brought their folk music—spirituals, work songs, and *blues*. Blues are pop-

ular songs about sadness or loneliness. The music used B-flat and E-flat in the scale, called *blue notes*. The music of the blacks got mixed with styles of music that were popular with the Spanish and French people. There was much musical activity in and around New Orleans, including street-singing, brass bands that played for parades and funerals, and popular music in nightclubs.

An early form of jazz, called *ragtime*, became popular in the early 1900's. The rhythm was fast and sometimes stressed a weak instead of a strong beat, giving the music a kind of "jerk." This is called *syncopation*, and is an important part of jazz. Ragtime enjoyed a revival in the 1970's, especially in the music of Scott Joplin. "The Entertainer," "Tiger Rag," and other songs are still popular.

Many musicians, white as well as black, were playing the new music. It began to be played in other big cities in the South, such as Atlanta, St. Louis, and Memphis. Chicago finally became the center for this music, with Joe "King" Oliver, Louis Armstrong, and others moving there from New Orleans. One group from Chicago went to New York in January 1917. Called the Original Dixieland Jazz Band, they were a great hit and soon made the first phonograph recording of jazz. This new, exciting

music was well liked, and the 1920's were called "The Jazz Age."

Changes in Jazz A smoother jazz style, called *swing*, became popular in the 1930's. This was played by big bands, especially those of Glenn Miller, Tommy and Jimmy Dorsey, and Benny Goodman. Swing was followed in the 1940's by *bebop* or *bop* (which used different rhythms and harmonies to play well-known tunes). Thelonius Monk was one of several jazz musicians who, in *jam sessions* (informal gatherings of musicians), developed bop.

Since the 1920's, jazz music has become popular all over the world. Composers of great symphonies and concert works have used jazz and jazz ideas in their creations. Duke Ellington wrote serious sacred jazz music and performed it in concert halls and churches. Three prominent jazz

▲ *Duke Ellington, composer, bandleader, and pianist* (above). *Thelonius Monk, composer and pianist* (left).

◄ *Ella Fitzgerald and Louis Armstrong, both brilliant jazz singers. Armstrong was also a great trumpet player.*

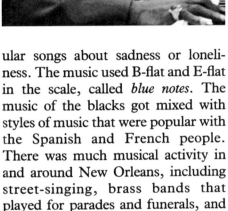

▲ *The original Dixieland Jazz Band. In 1917, they made the first jazz recording.*

groups, the Dave Brubeck Quartet, the Modern Jazz Quartet, and the Gerry Mulligan Quartet, have played jazz throughout the world. Many colleges offer jazz courses.

Instruments of Jazz Early jazz *combos* (instrumental music groups) featured the trumpet, trombone, and clarinet to play the melody. Drums, string bass, piano, and guitar or banjo kept the rhythm going. Saxophones and other instruments have also been added.

Appreciating Jazz An important part of jazz is *improvisation* (impromptu playing by a solo instrumentalist who is backed up by the other musicians). Jazz is unlike classical music and popular music because the improvisation makes it different every time it is played. When you listen to

jazz, you don't know what is going to happen next and you don't know what to expect. As they play, the musicians aim to be daring and to think up all kinds of musical ideas to make the music exciting. At the same time, they also play to drive the beat forward and make the music as lively as possible. If you like jazz, you will find that the music carries you along with it and is really involving. Good jazz is, as a famous jazz writer once put it, "the sound of surprise."

ALSO READ: ARMSTRONG, LOUIS; BRASS INSTRUMENTS; HANDY, W. C.; JACKSON, MAHALIA; PERCUSSION INSTRUMENTS.

JEFFERSON, THOMAS (1743–1826) Twenty-five years before he became President, Thomas Jefferson was the principal author of the Declaration of Independence. Two years before that, he had written *A Summary View of the Rights of British America*, protesting laws passed by the British Parliament.

"Let no law be passed by any one legislature," he wrote, "which may infringe on [step on] the rights and liberties of another. . . . The God who gave us life gave us liberty at the same time."

Thomas Jefferson was born at Shadwell, a farm in western Virginia.

Thomas Jefferson learned languages very easily. During his lifetime, he mastered Greek, Latin, Spanish, French, Anglo-Saxon, and Gaelic. He used to study for 15 hours a day, and then take a 2-mile (3-km) run.

THOMAS JEFFERSON
THIRD PRESIDENT   MARCH 4, 1801–MARCH 3, 1809

Born: April 13, 1743, Goochland County, Virginia (now Albemarle County)
Parents: Peter and Jane Randolph Jefferson
Education: William and Mary College, Williamsburg, Virginia
Religion: Deism (belief in God but not in any organized religion)
Occupation: Lawyer and writer
Political Party: Democratic-Republican
State Represented: Virginia
Married: 1772 to Martha Wayles Skelton (1748–1782)
Children: 5 daughters, 3 of whom died in childhood
Died: July 4, 1826, Monticello, Charlottesville, Virginia
Buried: Monticello, Charlottesville, Virginia

He was a brilliant student. He attended William and Mary College, where he read books by great English and French authors who wrote about liberty for all people. This was not a common belief in those days. After Jefferson graduated from college, he studied law. He became a member of the Virginia legislature and was a delegate to the Continental Congress in 1775. The Continental Congress adopted the Declaration of Independence, which Jefferson largely wrote. When the Congress ended, Jefferson returned to Virginia.

When Virginia was an English colony, a law had been passed that forbade people to attend any church except the Church of England. Jefferson suggested a new law to the state legislature, stating that "all men should be free to have their own religious opinions and that people should not be molested [harmed], restrained, or . . . otherwise made to suffer on account of their beliefs."

Jefferson also felt that slavery was wrong. He believed that a person had the right to freedom no matter what his or her abilities, education, or social status might be. He tried to keep slavery out of the new lands that were added to the United States. Despite his attitude toward slavery, Jefferson owned slaves all his life. But he left instructions that they were to be freed after he died.

Jefferson served his country as minister to France (1785–1789), as secretary of state (1790–1793), and as Vice-President (1797–1801). Jefferson became President in 1801. Soon afterward, his ministers in France made an agreement with the French government to buy the vast region between the Mississippi River and the Rocky Mountains. This was called the "Louisiana Purchase." It doubled the size of the United States. Jefferson was curious to know more about this huge area of western land. He sent the Lewis and Clark Expedition to explore this territory all the way to the Pacific Ocean.

No President ever had more varied interests and talents. He loved horseback riding, and even in his last years he rode as often as he could. Jefferson was not only a musician and a fine writer, but he was also an architect and inventor. He designed Monticello, his beautiful home near Charlottesville, Virginia. You can still visit it today and see his various inventions. Jefferson also founded the University of Virginia and designed the original buildings, which still stand. He set up a telescope at Monticello to watch those first buildings being built. Visitors to Monticello can still see the university through Jefferson's telescope. Jefferson arranged for good students from poor families to be admitted to the university free. At Monticello, where he spent his last seventeen years, Jefferson tried new ways to improve his crops.

During his lifetime, Jefferson saw his new nation successfully carrying out the ideals that had inspired the Declaration of Independence. "All eyes," he wrote, "are opened or opening to the rights of man." He wrote those words a few days before he died. The words Jefferson wrote for his own tombstone tell us the accomplishments of which he was most proud: "Here lies buried Thomas Jefferson, author of the Declaration of Independence, of the Statute of Virginia for Religious Freedom, and father of the University of Virginia." He did not mention the many government offices that he had held.

ALSO READ: AMERICAN REVOLUTION, CONTINENTAL CONGRESS, DECLARATION OF INDEPENDENCE, LEWIS AND CLARK EXPEDITION, LOUISIANA PURCHASE.

JELLYFISH Have you ever seen a jellyfish washed up on a beach? It is hard to believe that an animal that looks like a blob of jelly can give such

▲ *Monticello, Thomas Jefferson's home in Charlottesville, Virginia. This fine building was designed by Jefferson himself, as were many objects in it. It is now open to visitors.*

When Thomas Jefferson became president, 20 percent of the people in the United States were slaves. There were only five million inhabitants in all.

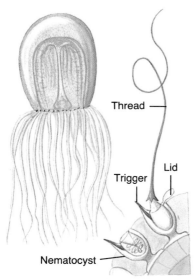

▲ *The poisonous sting of a jellyfish comes from tiny nematocysts on its tentacles. When triggered, each nematocyst shoots out its poisonous thread.*

About 98 percent of a jellyfish is water.

a painful sting. Some jellyfish do not sting, but the sting of others may be fatal (cause death).

A jellyfish, or medusa, is a simple, primitive sea animal. Its body is only two cell layers thick. Between these two cell walls is jelly. The jelly acts as a float to keep the animal near the water's surface. Jellyfish are often washed up onto beaches after storms or high tides.

The main part of a jellyfish's body looks like an umbrella. Hanging down from the umbrella are stringlike tentacles. In the tentacles are tiny cells (*nematocysts*) that contain a small amount of paralyzing poison. If a fish brushes against a jellyfish's tentacle, the nematocysts "explode," shooting poison into the victim. Then the tentacles pull the victim up to the mouth, at the bottom of the umbrella.

Jellyfish are *coelenterates*, water animals having a simple "stomach" with only one opening. Many coelenterates need two generations to complete a life cycle. The first generation is the free-swimming jellyfish. From the jellyfish's eggs come tiny *polyps*, ani-

▼ *The Portuguese man-of-war is not a single animal but a cluster of many small polyps under a gas-filled blue or pink float.*

mals that cling to rocks or plants on the ocean floor. The polyps then produce a third generation, which are jellyfish again.

One of the most common of the many types of jellyfish is the *moon jelly.* Another type that is found in many areas is the *sea nettle,* which often bothers swimmers with its stings. The world's largest jellyfish is the *Arctic sea blubber* that lives in the cold waters of the north. It may grow to be about 7 feet (2 m) across and have tentacles more than 100 feet (30 m) long. The kind of sea blubber that lives in warmer waters is only about a foot (30 cm) across. Its tentacles often give swimmers painful stings.

The most famous jellyfish is the *Portuguese man-of-war.* This is not a true jellyfish, but a colony of animals. It is a beautiful purple-blue color, with dangerous tentacles often over 60 feet (18 m) long.

ALSO READ: COELENTERATE, CORAL.

JENNER, EDWARD (1749–1823) An English doctor, Edward Jenner, discovered a vaccine to protect people from smallpox. As a result of Jenner's discovery, smallpox—which was one of mankind's worst enemies—has almost disappeared.

Jenner noticed that people who got the mild disease cowpox never got that disease again, nor did they ever get smallpox. (Both cowpox and smallpox produce large pimplelike sores all over a person's body.) Jenner thought about this strange fact and decided that if a person were purposely given cowpox, then that person would not get smallpox.

On May 14, 1796, Jenner took some pus from a cowpox sore on the arm of a milkmaid. He made a small cut in the arm of an eight-year-old boy, and rubbed cowpox pus into the cut. This was the first vaccination. Four weeks after the boy recovered from cowpox, Jenner rubbed smallpox pus into a cut in the boy's arm. The boy did not get smallpox.

At first, other doctors showed no interest in Jenner's discovery, but before his death, Jenner was honored throughout the world as the conqueror of the dreaded smallpox. Other doctors, using Jenner's ideas, have developed vaccines to protect people from many other diseases.

ALSO READ: DISEASE, IMMUNITY.

JERUSALEM Jerusalem is among the oldest cities in the world and has played a leading role in history. Jews, Christians, and Muslims consider it a holy city. Jerusalem lies about 35 miles (56 km) from the Mediterranean Sea in the Judean hills on Israel's eastern border with Jordan. It is the capital of Israel and has a population of 432,000 people.

Jerusalem was an important city when King David of the Jews made it his capital around 1000 B.C. His son, King Solomon, built a great temple there. The Jews held the city for about 500 years but were then conquered by the Babylonians. The Romans occupied the city in 65 B.C. About 90 years later, Jesus Christ was tried there by the Roman governor, Pontius Pilate, and was crucified. The Jews revolted against the harsh Roman rule in A.D. 66, and the Roman Emperor, Titus, destroyed the city and the temple. Constantine, the first Christian Roman emperor, rebuilt Jerusalem in the A.D. 300's. He built the Church of the Holy Sepulcher on the spot where Christ was believed to have been buried.

Muslim Arabs conquered the city in A.D. 637. They believed that their greatest teacher, Muhammad, rose to heaven from the same spot where King Solomon's temple once stood. They built the Dome of the Rock, an important shrine, on the site.

Muslim Arabs, Christian Crusad-ers, Turks, and finally the British occupied the city in the hundreds of years before 1948. When the State of Israel was established that year, West Jerusalem became the capital of Israel. East Jerusalem, controlled by Jordan, was taken by Israel during the Six-Day, or Arab-Israeli, War of June, 1967. Today, some countries do not recognize Israeli control of all Jerusalem.

Jerusalem today is a fascinating mixture of old and new, East and West. The historical area of the city, now called the "Old City," is surrounded by a huge stone wall built by a Turkish sultan in the 1500's. This area's narrow cobblestone streets teem with colorful activity. Most of Jerusalem's great religious landmarks are located in the Old City. Jews worship at the Wailing Wall, the remains of King Solomon's great temple. Christians visit the Church of the Holy Sepulcher, built over the tomb of Christ. Muslims visit the Dome of the Rock. The so-called "New City" consists of modern apartments and office buildings built outside the Old City's walls. Interesting sights here include Hebrew University, the Orthodox Jewish quarter, and King David's Tomb on Mount Zion.

ALSO READ: CHRISTIANITY, ISLAM, ISRAEL, JEWISH HISTORY, JORDAN, JUDAISM, MIDDLE EAST.

▲ *Edward Jenner, who discovered vaccination.*

The word "vaccination" comes from *vaccinia*, another name for cowpox.

▼ *Jerusalem is a holy city for Jews, Christians, and Muslims. The picture shows the Dome of the Rock and the Wailing Wall in front of it. Jews gather at the wall to pray.*

The New Testament of the Bible was written in the days of the Roman Empire. It covers a period from the reign of King Herod to the fall of Jerusalem in A.D. 70. The first four books—Matthew, Mark, Luke, and John—were written soon after the death of Jesus, and probably before A.D. 100.

▼ *Jesus is often depicted performing the miracles described in the Bible. Here, he makes a blind beggar see again.*

JESUS CHRIST (about 4 B.C.–about A.D. 29) Christianity was founded on the teachings of Jesus Christ. Much of our knowledge of Jesus comes from the writings of the New Testament of the Bible. The parts that tell the story of Jesus are the Gospels (from the Old English words, Good Spiel, meaning "good news") of Matthew, Mark, Luke, and John. The good news these writers wanted to tell was that Jesus is the Christ, the son of God, and to explain his ideas. This may be why they tell us so little about the life story of Jesus. The Gospels appeared 35 to 70 years after Jesus' death.

Jesus comes from a Hebrew word meaning "God is Salvation." Christ comes from a Greek word translating the Hebrew word "Messiah"—the anointed (chosen) one. The name Jesus Christ expresses the faith of the early Christians that Jesus is the Messiah, or Savior.

▲ *An early painting showing the baptism of Christ. This work of art hangs in the National Gallery of Art, Washington, D.C.*

Jesus was born to a devout Jewish couple in the ancient country of Judea (now parts of Israel and Jordan). According to the Gospels, Jesus' mother, Mary, was told by an angel that she would give birth to the son of God. Soon afterwards, Mary was married to Joseph of Nazareth, a carpenter. Joseph and Mary traveled to the little town of Bethlehem to register for a tax list. The small town was so crowded that the only room left for them was a stable. It was there in the stable that the baby Jesus was born.

Little is known about the early years of Jesus' life. The Gospels agree that Jesus probably began preaching at about the age of 30. He chose 12 of his followers to be his apostles and help him in his work. Jesus was a good speaker and storyteller, and he attracted huge crowds of people. The Gospels tell how he could make sick people well with the power of faith and could make miracles happen. He taught people that God is our father and that we are brothers and should love one another as God loves us. He taught that God forgives people to the degree that they forgive one another, and that God will grant them eternal life.

Fear on the part of civil and reli-

gious authorities of what Jesus said and did led to his arrest in Jerusalem. He was brought to trial. Pontius Pilate, the Roman governor, sentenced him to die on the cross. (Crucifixion was a common form of execution at that time.) At the Last Supper, the night before he died, Jesus celebrated the Passover feast with his disciples. As he gave them bread and wine, Jesus said, "This is my body," and "This is my blood." He told them to eat bread and drink wine in the same manner after his death and resurrection. From this simple act originated the Christian sacrament of Holy Communion, commemorating the death of Christ.

After Jesus died, his body was placed in a tomb. On the third day afterward, the tomb was found open, and Jesus was gone. The Gospels report that he appeared to several of his followers after he had risen from the dead. He was with his disciples until the day that they saw him taken up into heaven.

The Gospel or "good news" of Jesus' resurrection and his teachings were carried first to the Jews and then to the Gentiles (non-Jews). The early Christians often met in synagogues in Palestine. For a long time Christianity was considered to be part of Judaism. His followers took his teachings to other people and other nations. Christianity became one of the major religions of the world. The calendar in use today is dated from the time of the birth of Jesus. "B.C." means "before Christ." "A.D." stands for *anno domini* (in the year of our Lord) and is used for dates after Christ's birth.

ALSO READ: BIBLE, CHRISTIANITY, CHRISTMAS, EASTER, RELIGION.

▲ *Jesus calling Peter and Andrew to serve him and become his first disciples. Jesus filled their net with fish after they had fished all night without success.*

Although the Christian calendar is dated from the year of Christ's birth, no one is quite sure of the exact year in which Christ was born. It is thought to have been between 4 B.C. and 7 B.C. The Bible says that Jesus was born during the reign of King Herod, and we know that Herod died about 4 B.C. It is also thought that the census, which was the reason why Joseph and Mary went to Bethlehem, took place in 6 B.C.

▼ *This dramatic painting of the death of Christ is called* Lamentation over the Dead Christ. *It was painted about 1500 by the Italian painter Botticelli.*

JET PROPULSION The words "jet propulsion" usually describe how many kinds of airplanes move. When you blow up a balloon and let it go, it zooms around the room because it is also jet-propelled. Sir Isaac Newton explained how jets—and balloons—move when he said, "For every action, there is an equal and opposite reaction." This is called the Third Law of Motion. You can see how it explains what happens to the balloon. Air rushes out through the neck of the balloon (action), and the balloon moves in the opposite direction (reaction).

A jet-propelled airplane is more complicated, but the idea is the same. The engine is a long tube. At the front of the tube is a powerful fan that sucks in air into a *compressor*. The compressor pushes the air to the *combustion chamber*, where fuel (kerosene) is sprayed into the air. When the engine is first turned on, a spark causes the fuel to burn. After that, the fuel burns as soon as it is sprayed into the combustion chamber. The engine stops when the fuel is cut off.

The heated air expands very rapidly. The only direction the air can move is backward, toward the open end of the tube. The rush of hot air from the back of the engine creates a reaction force (thrust) on the engine in the opposite direction. This causes the forward movement of the airplane.

Near the back of the jet engine is a *turbine*, another special fan. The hot air spins the turbine as it rushes past. The turbine is connected to the compressor, so more air is pulled into the engine.

A jet engine gets oxygen for burning fuel from the outside air. This means that it can work only in the atmosphere. A rocket engine, which produces a jet of hot gas, may carry its own oxygen, allowing it to burn fuel in space, where there is no atmosphere.

ALSO READ: AIRPLANE; ENGINE; MOTION; NEWTON, SIR ISAAC; ROCKET.

JET STREAM see ATMOSPHERE.

JEWELRY Some experts think the word "jewelry" comes from the French word *joie*, meaning "joy" or "gladness." People have always decorated themselves with beautiful things to make themselves look attractive or important. Long ago, people fastened

Long ago, in the first century A.D., a Greek mathematician named Hero made the first jet engine. He suspended a hollow metal ball containing water. When he boiled the water, the steam escaped through two nozzles, one on either side of the ball. Because the nozzles pointed in opposite directions, the force of the escaping steam made the ball spin.

The simplest type of jet engines are ramjets. They have no fans or turbines—air is just squeezed into the tube as it moves through the air.

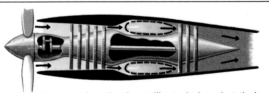

Turboprop engines produce jet thrust like turbojets, but their turbines also drive a propeller. They are more economical but slower than pure jets, and were popular for transport aircraft.

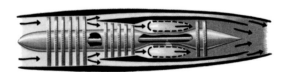

Bypass (or turbofan) jet engines have huge fans at the front to suck in vast amounts of air. Some of this bypasses the combustion chamber and then rejoins the exhaust gases. The result is much greater thrust.

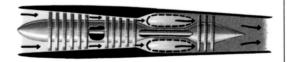

Turbojets are noisier and less powerful than turbofans, but they were long preferred for warplanes because they are smaller and easy to fit with afterburners.

pretty things on their heads, around their necks and arms, or in their noses and ears. Seashells, animal teeth, carved bone, and birds' feathers made decorations for happy celebrations. Warriors often wore similar decorations to raise their spirits before a battle. People living near the sea used shells for jewelry. They discovered pearls in oysters. They also learned how to cut and polish the stones from the ground into beautifully colored gems.

The early Egyptians were familiar with many precious and semiprecious gems. They used amber, amethyst, and crystal in their jewelry, as well as colored glass. The ancient Greeks considered gold to be more valuable than gemstones. Their heavy decorations were mostly made of gold, but sometimes they would add a bit of enamel or a few pearls. The people of South Africa became expert at making delicate gold wire jewelry. An ancient skeleton found in Ecuador in South America has small gold circles set into five of its front teeth.

Greek culture began to spread to Rome about 200 B.C. An important

Roman statesman, named Cato, thought the Greek love of decoration would ruin his people. He passed laws limiting jewelry. The Romans then began having ordinary things, such as hairpins and mirrors, made by jewelers.

In more recent times, French, English, and Italian craftworkers have raised jewelry-making to a real art. Royal crown jewels of various countries are perhaps the finest examples of their work.

In former times, all jewelry was made by hand. Now machines can do some of the work. If manufacturers want to make several bracelets that are all alike, they use a method called *casting*. First, a model of the bracelet is made out of metal, and this model is covered with melted rubber. When the rubber hardens, it is carefully removed. This makes a rubber mold of the bracelet. A wax model of the bracelet is made with the rubber mold. The wax model is then covered with plaster and put in an oven. As the heat melts the wax model inside the plaster, the wax drains out through a small hole. Then the precious metal, such as gold, silver, or platinum, is poured into the plaster mold through the small hole and allowed to harden. When the plaster is

▲ *A scarf dancer from Hong Kong displays elaborate jewelry worn as part of her costume.*

▼ *Three brooches that would have been worn by a Viking woman. The two oval ones are bronze and are about 4 inches (10 cm) long. The third brooch would have been used to fasten a shawl.*

▼ *This elegant necklace from China is made of pieces of carved jade. It dates from several centuries before Christ's birth.*

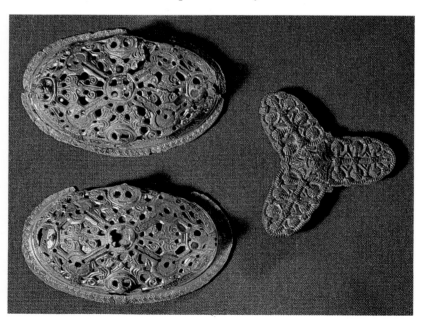

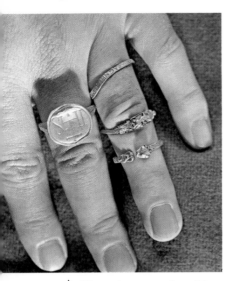

▲ *These rings were found by deep-sea divers along with other treasures from the Spanish Armada. The ship they were on sank off the British coast in 1588.*

removed, the bracelet is polished.

Jewelry is also made by *stamping*. A flat sheet of precious metal is pressed between two curved pieces of steel, called *dies*. The dies shape the metal into the form of a bracelet, a ring, or whatever is being made. The stamping method is used for very large amounts of jewelry of the same pattern.

Many people wear *costume jewelry*, which is made of less valuable stones or glass and less expensive metals. Some attractive costume jewelry is made of plastic.

■ LEARN BY DOING

You can make colorful jewelry of your own. Use materials such as interesting pasta shapes—paint them and string them like beads. Homemade clay beads are fun, too. You can get special clay that can be painted and hardened in the oven. Make a necklace from colorful drinking straws by cutting them into short lengths. Try making paper beads: Cut out colorful shiny pages from old magazines, and cut them up into long, slim triangles. Roll the triangles tightly, wide end first, around a thin knitting needle. Glue the pointed end down to hold it. Slide the bead off the knitting needle. Varnish the beads and thread them to make a necklace. ■

ALSO READ: CROWN JEWELS, GEM.

JEWISH HISTORY The history of a country, or the people of a nation, is a record of events in the development of that country. Jewish history is even more—it is the thread that has bound the Jewish people together through thousands of years of persecution, owning no land, and wandering.

The Origins of the Jewish People
The Old Testament, the first half of the Bible, tells of the beginnings of

▲ *Moses, the prophet and lawgiver, carved in marble by Michelangelo. The Bible says that God gave Moses the Ten Commandments on Mount Sinai.*

the Jews, of their wanderings, and of their establishment of a homeland. The Biblical word "Hebrew" refers to a group of wandering tribes that lived in the Middle East before 1300 B.C. In those days, most people worshiped many gods, who were often represented in statues. But the Hebrews were *monotheistic*, believing that there was only one true God. The word "Jew" originally meant "a member of the Hebrew tribe of Judah," or "a member of the Hebrew state, Judea."

Both the Old Testament and historical theory trace the ancestors of the Jews to the ancient city of Ur in Mesopotamia. About 2350 B.C., Abraham, a tribal chief who was told by God that he would be the "father of a multitude," made a *covenant*, or agreement, with God. If Abraham and his descendants would worship only this God and follow his laws, God would lead them into "a land of milk and honey" and they would prosper. Abraham led his followers to Canaan in what is now Israel.

Isaac was the son of Abraham, and Jacob was the son of Isaac. God spoke to Jacob, telling him that he would become known as "Israel," and his descendants would be the "children of Israel." Jacob's (Israel's) twelve sons and their descendants formed the twelve Hebrew tribes that became the Jewish people.

▼ *David, the second king of Israel, praying in his old age.*

Promised Land Won—and Lost

About 1700 B.C., some Hebrew tribes wandered to the borders of Egypt. There they prospered for over 100 years. Then they were forced into slavery by the Egyptians. According to the Bible, a Hebrew prophet named Moses forced the Egyptian pharaoh to free the Hebrew slaves. Moses led the Hebrews out of Egypt, and they became desert wanderers. During this period of wandering, Moses received the Ten Commandments from God.

The Bible says that the Hebrews wandered over the desert for 40 years. In the 1200's B.C., they settled in Canaan. There, about 1030 B.C., they founded a kingdom. The greatest kings were Saul, David, and David's son, Solomon. The great temple in Jerusalem was built during the reign of Solomon.

When Solomon died, the kingdom was divided. Ten tribes formed a northern kingdom called Israel. The remaining two tribes created a southern kingdom, Judah.

In the 700's B.C., the kingdom of Israel was invaded by the Assyrians, and Israel was destroyed. The ten tribes living there were scattered over the world, and came to be known as the "Lost Tribes of Israel."

In 597 B.C., the kingdom of Judah was attacked by the Babylonians. Most Judeans were taken to Babylon, where they lived in exile.

When the Persian Empire conquered Babylon about 539 B.C., the Jews there were allowed to go home. The temple in Jerusalem was rebuilt, and Judah prospered. Around this time, Jews formed colonies throughout the Mediterranean and Black Sea areas. This great movement was called the "Diaspora," or *dispersion* (scattering).

In the 330's B.C., Alexander the Great of Macedonia conquered the Persian Empire. After Alexander's death, Judah was ruled by Egypt, and later by Syria. The Jews were forbidden to practice their religion, and an alter to Zeus (the supreme Greek god) was placed in Solomon's Temple. A rebellion of the Jews was led by a Jewish priest and his sons, who were called the Macabees. After a bitter military struggle, the Jewish forces defeated Syria. Judah was briefly free again.

In 47 B.C., Judah was made a province of the Roman Empire. The Roman governors of Judah gave little respect to the Jewish religion. In A.D. 70, the temple of Jerusalem was again destroyed. Judah was finally crushed in A.D. 135. The Jews no longer had a homeland.

The total of world Jewry is estimated at about 17 million. The United States has more Jews than any other country, with about 2 million in the New York area alone. The total in Israel is about 3½ million.

A number of Jews sailed with Columbus on his first voyage to the New World. Some accounts say that a Jew named Luis de Torres was the first man to step onto American soil.

▲ *Chaim Weizmann's inauguration as the first president of the State of Israel on February 17, 1949.*

▼ *A gilded statue of Joan of Arc in the Place des Pyramides in Paris reminds the French of their great heroine.*

Persecution and Hope In the centuries following the loss of their homeland, the Jewish people were persecuted wherever they went. There were periods of peaceful prosperity. Then some internal strife would upset the country, and the Jews would sometimes be blamed as the cause of problems. In the Middle Ages, Christian countries in Europe were especially cruel to Jews.

When the Jews were allowed to remain in a country, they were often forced to live in small, crowded areas, called *ghettos*, and to wear special clothing. They were not allowed to vote, own land, or practice any profession. During the 1200's and 1300's, several European kings filled their treasuries by taking things that belonged to the Jews.

For several centuries in Spain, colonies of Jews lived peacefully under the rule of Spanish Muslims or Moors. Many Spanish Jews were government officials, lawyers, bankers, doctors, and scholars. When the Muslims were driven from Spain in the 1200's, this peaceful period ended.

In 1480, the Spanish Inquisition was established in Spain. This court—independent of the Church—persecuted persons suspected of heresy (not believing in the doctrines of the Church). In order to save their lives, many Jews converted to Christianity, while secretly practicing Judaism. But all Jews were finally banished from Spain in 1492.

Thousands of Spanish Jews migrated to Turkey, which still followed the Muslim policy of toleration. Jews were expelled from England, France, Germany, and Switzerland and settled in Poland and Russia. In the 1600's and 1700's, Jews were again welcomed in England and France. Many also sought refuge in the new colonies in North America. But in Russia and Poland, terrible massacres (*pogroms*) of entire Jewish villages began. In the centuries of wandering, the Jewish people in every land retained their identity as Jews by maintaining their faith. They waited for the coming of a Messiah who would again lead them to the promised land.

The Homeland Regained In 1896, an Austrian named Theodor Herzl founded a movement called *Zionism*. The aim of this movement was to regain the Jewish homeland in the Middle East and reestablish the Jewish nation. Meanwhile, a wave of hatred against Jews, called *anti-Semitism*, was rising in Europe. In the 1930's and early 1940's, the German dictator, Adolf Hitler, and his Nazi followers murdered about six million Jews in Germany and German-occupied countries.

In 1948, the State of Israel was established in Palestine. Once again, all Jews had a homeland. Israel is also the home of many Arabs and Christians. Today, there are about 17 million Jews throughout the world. Many of them (over seven million) live in North America. Israel and the Soviet Union also have large Jewish populations.

ALSO READ: BABYLONIA; BIBLE; DEAD SEA SCROLLS; EGYPT, ANCIENT; HANUKKAH; HEBREW; ISRAEL; JERUSALEM; JUDAISM; MIDDLE EAST; PALESTINE; PASSOVER; YIDDISH LANGUAGE.

JOAN OF ARC (1412–1431) "I will teach them all to fight that the will of God may be done in France." These words were spoken by Joan of Arc in *Saint Joan*, a play written by dramatist George Bernard Shaw.

Joan of Arc, or Jeanne d'Arc, was a young French girl who led her people to victory in battle with the English. She was born in Domrémy, France, to a peasant family. At the age of 13, Joan had visions and heard voices that she said were from heaven. The voices told her she must help free the French from the English. At this time, the English controlled part of France.

Joan went to see Charles (later King Charles VII), the uncrowned leader of the French people. He became convinced Joan had powers given to her by heaven. He put her in charge of his troops. Joan freed the city of Orléans from the English in May 1429. After that, she was known as the Maid of Orléans. When Charles was crowned king, Joan had the place of honor at his side.

In 1430, allies of the English, the Burgundians, captured Joan and sold her to the English. The English put her on trial as a witch. She was found guilty and was burned at the stake in Rouen, France. Joan was declared a saint by the Roman Catholic Church in 1920.

Some of the plays about Joan of Arc (besides *Saint Joan*) include *The Maid of Orléans* by Johann Friedrich von Schiller, *The Lark* by Jean Anouilh, and *Joan of Lorraine* by Maxwell Anderson. Mark Twain wrote a historical novel about her, called *The Personal Recollections of Joan of Arc*.

ALSO READ: CHARLES, KINGS OF FRANCE; FRENCH HISTORY; HUNDRED YEARS' WAR; SAINT.

JOGGING see EXERCISE.

JOHN, KING OF ENGLAND (1167–1216) King John of England was an unpopular king, and his enemies called him cruel and dishonest. As the youngest son of King Henry II, he received no lands from his father, and so he was called John Lackland. But his older brother, who had inherited the throne as King Richard I, gave John much English land. John tried to take the crown from his brother while Richard was a prisoner in Austria. Richard had been imprisoned on his way back to England after the Third Crusade. Richard forgave John and supposedly made him heir to the throne. John became king after Richard died in 1199.

The kings of England once ruled over several provinces in France. John lost most of these provinces in a long war with the French king. John also quarreled with the pope. The pope sided with John's greatest enemies, the English *barons* (noblemen). John had forced the barons to pay for the French war with huge taxes. He refused to listen to their complaints. In 1215, the barons presented the *Magna Carta* (the Great Charter) to King John at Runnymede. John was forced to sign this historic document, which limited the power of the king and gave the barons certain rights. John then went to war against the barons, in spite of the agreements he had made in the Magna Carta. The struggle ended with John's sudden death. His nine-year-old son became King Henry III.

ALSO READ: CRUSADES; ENGLISH HISTORY; KINGS AND QUEENS; MAGNA CARTA; RICHARD, KINGS OF ENGLAND.

JOHNSON, ANDREW (1809–1875) Andrew Johnson was the Vice-President who became President when Abraham Lincoln was assassinated in 1865. He inherited all the problems of Lincoln's administration. Lincoln had wanted to show understanding and mercy to the South after the Civil War. President Johnson wanted to do the same thing. He was strongly opposed by certain Republicans in Congress who insisted that the Confederate states be punished. Harsh laws were passed, even though Johnson had *vetoed* (rejected) them. The quarrel between Congress and the President became so bitter that the House of Representatives voted to *impeach* him. This means the House accused him of wrongdoing,

Joan of Arc said she was guided by the visions and voices of three saints whose statues stood in her village church. Some doctors think she simply suffered from a complaint that made her see and hear things.

▲ *King John of England.*

ANDREW JOHNSON
SEVENTEENTH PRESIDENT   APRIL 15, 1865–MARCH 4, 1869

Born: December 29, 1808, Raleigh, North Carolina
Parents: Jacob and Mary McDonough Johnson
Education: Mostly self-educated
Religion: No special church
Occupation: Tailor
Political Party: National Union-Republican
State Represented: Tennessee
Married: 1827 to Eliza McCardle (1810–1876)
Children: 2 daughters, 3 sons
Died: July 31, 1875, Carter's Station, Tennessee
Buried: National Cemetery, Greeneville, Tennessee

▲ *The reasons for impeaching President Andrew Johnson are presented to the Senate by Senator Thaddeus Stevens.*

hoping to force him out of office. The Senate, however, found him innocent of the charges. Johnson was the only President who has ever been impeached.

Johnson was born in Raleigh, North Carolina, to very poor parents. He never attended school. At age 14, he became an apprentice (student and helper) to a tailor. At 18, he moved to the town of Greeneville, Tennessee, where he set up his own tailor shop. He married Eliza McCardle, a school-teacher, and she taught him to read and write. She also read aloud to him while he stitched clothes for his customers.

Young Johnson was both well liked and eager to get ahead. He became interested in politics and was elected mayor of Greeneville. He was later elected to more important offices and was serving as U.S. Senator from Tennessee when the Civil War began. Tennessee left the Union to fight for the South, but Johnson remained loyal to the United States. In 1864, Lincoln asked him to run for Vice-President. The two men were from different political parties, but they were elected together on the National Union ticket.

Less than two years after Johnson became President, the impeachment trial began. It was held in the Senate and, according to the Constitution, a two-thirds vote would be needed to

convict him. After several months, the Senate failed by one vote to convict Johnson. He finished his term as President.

In 1875, Johnson returned to Washington as a senator from Tennessee. At that time, many Americans felt that the charges against him in the impeachment trial had been false ones, made up by his political enemies. Johnson gave a speech in the Senate, denouncing the spirit of hate that he feared might still wreck the Union. And he urged his fellow Senators to concentrate on "this grand work of saving the Constitution," which meant "saving the country." He said, "Let peace and prosperity be restored to the land." Johnson died a few weeks later.

ALSO READ: CIVIL WAR; IMPEACHMENT; LINCOLN, ABRAHAM.

JOHNSON, LYNDON BAINES
(1908–1973) The thirty-sixth President of the United States took the oath of office in an unusual place—aboard an Air Force jet. Lyndon Johnson was the Vice-President under President John F. Kennedy. Johnson was in Dallas, Texas, with the President on November 22, 1963, the day Kennedy was assassinated. Less than two hours after Kennedy died, Johnson was sworn in as Presi-

dent by a woman who was a federal judge. The ceremony was held on the jet plane that carried Johnson back to Washington, D.C.

Lyndon Baines Johnson, often called "LBJ," was born and grew up in central Texas. Johnson taught high school for two years after graduating from college. He then went to Washington to work as a congressional secretary. LBJ returned to Texas in 1935 to become a state administrator of the National Youth Administration. He helped many needy young people find work during the Depression when there were very few jobs. Two years later, Johnson was elected to the U.S. Congress as a representative from Texas.

Johnson served in the House of Representatives for 11 years. In 1948, he was elected to the Senate, where he became known as "the man who gets things done." He served as the Democratic Party whip, or assistant leader, and later became the majority leader. Johnson won the Democratic nomination for Vice-President in 1960.

After Johnson became President, he addressed a joint session of Congress. He suggested that the best way to honor the memory of John Kennedy was to pass bills the late President had requested. Johnson had great influence with the Congress, having served in both houses

for many years. During the next few months, civil rights, anti-poverty, and tax reduction bills were enacted into law. In 1964, Johnson was nominated by the Democrats for the Presidency. He received a larger majority vote in the election than any other President before him.

Mrs. Johnson—named Claudia Taylor but always called "Lady Bird"—campaigned actively with President Johnson. A favorite project of hers during his Presidency was beautification of the United States. She led a successful campaign to abolish billboards and junkyards and to plant flowers and trees along roads and parkways.

During Johnson's administration, more troops were sent to fight in Vietnam. Many Americans believed the war was unjust. The country became divided, and Johnson decided not to seek reelection.

▲ *President Lyndon Johnson talks with Russian Premier Aleksei Kosygin. The meeting, designed to further Soviet-American understanding, took place in Glassboro, New Jersey, in 1967.*

President Johnson was widely known by his initials, LBJ. These same initials applied to his family too. The President's wife was called Lady Bird Johnson, and their two daughters were Lynda Bird and Luci Baines. Even the family dogs were called Little Beagle Johnson and Little Beagle Junior!

LYNDON BAINES JOHNSON
THIRTY-SIXTH PRESIDENT   NOVEMBER 22, 1963–JANUARY 20, 1969

Born: August 27, 1908, Stonewall, Texas
Parents: Samuel Ealy, Jr., and Rebekah Baines Johnson
Education: Southwest Texas State Teachers College
Religion: Christian Church (Disciples of Christ)
Occupation: Teacher and legislator
Political Party: Democratic
State Represented: Texas
Married: 1934 to Claudia ("Lady Bird") Taylor (born 1912)
Children: 2 daughters
Died: January 22, 1973, LBJ Ranch, Stonewall, Texas
Buried: LBJ Ranch, Stonewall, Texas

▲ *Samuel Johnson, English writer and wit.*

Samuel Johnson first became famous when his great *Dictionary of the English Language* was published in 1755 after eight years' work. It set the style for all dictionaries from that day to this. Johnson was the first to explain the meanings of words with quotations. His example for the word "dull" was: "To make dictionaries is *dull* work."

▲ *John Paul Jones, a naval hero of the American Revolution.*

After the former President returned to his Texas ranch, he planned and contributed to the building of a huge library at the University of Texas. The Lyndon Baines Johnson Library and School of Public Affairs opened in 1971.

ALSO READ: CIVIL RIGHTS MOVEMENT; KENNEDY, JOHN FITZGERALD; VIETNAM; VIETNAM WAR.

JOHNSON, SAMUEL (1709–1774)
"Being in a ship is being in a jail, with the chance of being drowned." These words were spoken by Samuel Johnson, who was one of the wittiest writers of the 1700's.

Johnson was born in Staffordshire, England. His father was a bookseller, and Johnson received much of his early education from reading his father's books. He attended Oxford University for three years and ran a boys' school for a short time.

Johnson later moved to London, where he became well known for his writing and for his witty comments on people, literature, and life in general. His best-known work is the *Dictionary of the English Language*. It contains such humorous definitions as: "oats—a grain which in England is generally given to horses, but in Scotland supports the people." He also wrote a long poem, called *The Vanity of Human Wishes*, and a series of essays. A good judge of literature, he published *The Lives of the Most Eminent English Poets, with Critical Observations on Their Works*.

In 1763, Johnson met a young Scottish lawyer named James Boswell, who became his close friend and companion. Boswell kept a record of almost everything Johnson said and did. After Johnson's death, Boswell wrote *The Life of Samuel Johnson*, a biography that became a great work of literature in itself.

ALSO READ: LITERATURE.

JONES, JOHN PAUL (1747–1792)
"I have not yet begun to fight," declared John Paul Jones, an American naval hero. He made this famous reply when the captain of a British warship asked Jones to surrender his ship during a naval battle in the American Revolution.

John Paul Jones's real name was John Paul. He was born in Scotland. At the age of 12, he sailed to Virginia as a cabin boy aboard an English ship. He then began his career at sea, sailing on slave trading ships in the West Indies. After John was accused of murdering a man during a mutiny, he escaped to America. There he added Jones to his name to hide his identity.

When the American Revolution began, Jones became an officer in the colonial navy. He commanded the *Alfred*, the first naval vessel purchased by the Continental Congress. He captured many ships filled with valuable cargo, and his fame grew. Jones won his best-known battle with the British on September 23, 1779. His ship, the *Bonhomme Richard*, defeated the British ship, the *Serapis*. Congress later awarded Jones the only gold medal given to an officer in the colonial navy.

Jones went to Europe in 1783. He then served as an admiral in the Russian navy during that country's war against the Turks. He later moved to Paris, where he died.

ALSO READ: AMERICAN REVOLUTION.

JORDAN Jordan is a new kingdom but also an ancient land described in the Bible. Most of the country lies on a plateau approximately 3,000 feet (900 m) above sea level. The Jordan River and Dead Sea lie west of the plateau. Amman is the capital and largest city. (See the map with the article on the MIDDLE EAST.)

Jordan's climate has sharp seasonal variations. Temperatures below 39°F

JORDAN

Capital City: Amman (830,000 people).
Area: 37,738 square miles (97,734 sq. km).
Population: 3,000,000.
Government: Monarchy.
Natural Resources: Phosphate rock.
Export Products: Phosphate, fruit and vegetables.
Unit of Money: Dinar.
Official Language: Arabic.

(4°C) occur in January, the coldest month. August, the hottest, has an average temperature of 92°F (33°C). Rain falls mostly in the winter. The southern and eastern parts have a desert climate, with little rain.

Jordanians can cultivate only a small portion of the land because the climate is so dry. The principal crops are beans, peas, grains, citrus fruits, grapes, and bananas. Camels, cattle, and goats are herded.

Natural resources include manganese, iron, phosphates, and potash. Phosphates and potash are made into fertilizer. An oil pipeline, extending from Saudi Arabia to Lebanon, crosses Jordan. Jordanians work in oil refineries near Amman. They are also employed in food processing and leather tanning.

Jordan is an ancient land. It later became part of the Roman Empire until the Arabs pushed out the Romans. In the early 1500's, the Turks took over and held the region for approximately 400 years. The British controlled Jordanian territory after World War I. They recognized Jordan's independence in 1946, and Abdullah became the country's new king. Abdullah was assassinated in 1951 because he seemed to want peace with neighboring Israel, and his grandson, King Hussein, was crowned in 1952.

Ever since Israel became a separate country in 1948, the Jordanians and Israelis have been unfriendly neigh-bors. Many Arabs from Palestine (now called Israel) have been forced to live in Jordan. These Palestinians have brought great problems to Jordan. In June 1967, the Israelis captured Jordanian land west of the Jordan River. This land is called the West Bank and includes East Jerusalem where the Dome of the Rock is located. Most Jordanians, who are Muslims, believe that this shrine stands where the prophet Muhammad ascended to heaven. Today, many Israelis live on the West Bank. Arab demonstrations against these Israeli settlers have led to continual violence.

ALSO READ: ISLAM, ISRAEL, JERUSALEM, MIDDLE EAST.

▼ *Trees and shrubs line the banks of the Jordan River. According to the Bible, it was here that the Israelites crossed over into the Promised Land. Like much of this part of the Middle East, Jordan is steeped in Biblical history.*

▲ *Chief Joseph, Nez Percé Indian chief.*

▲ *A journalist at work in a busy newspaper office today has modern technology at his fingertips. He can type articles directly into a computer which sets the words as they will appear in the newspaper.*

JOSEPH, CHIEF (about 1840–1904) The last and most famous leader of the Nez Percé Indians was Chief Joseph. The Nez Percé lived in northeastern Oregon, where they fished for salmon, raised horses, and gathered roots and berries. They had welcomed the explorers Lewis and Clark to the Northwest in 1805.

By 1850, white settlers, miners, and gold seekers looked with longing eyes on the beautiful valleys of the Nez Percé. The U.S. government told Chief Joseph to move his people away from their homeland to a reservation in Idaho. But the Nez Percé had already given much of their land to the government. "The earth is our mother," said Joseph. "How can we sell you our mother?"

In 1873, President Ulysses S. Grant agreed that this land belonged to the Indians, but two years later he changed his mind. Chief Joseph refused to move. The U.S. Army was sent to force the tribe off their land. The peace-loving Nez Percé would have to leave—or fight.

Chief Joseph guided his braves to victory in the first two battles. But the soldiers greatly outnumbered the Indians. Joseph ordered a fighting retreat, seeking safety across the border in Canada. It was one of the most remarkable retreats in military history. The soldiers caught the Nez Percé after a 1,000-mile (1,600-km) chase. Few of the warriors were still alive. Joseph had to surrender— about 40 miles (65 km) south of the Canadian border. At the surrender, Joseph made a speech, ending with the words: "Hear me, my chiefs, I am tired; my heart is sick and sad. From where the sun now stands, I will fight no more forever."

ALSO READ: INDIANS, AMERICAN; NEZ PERCÉ INDIANS.

JOSEPH, SAINT see JESUS CHRIST.

JOSEPHINE see NAPOLEON BONAPARTE.

JOURNALISM How do you find out what happened on the other side of the world today? Or in a state a thousand miles away from where you live? Or even what happened in your own neighborhood? You probably look in a newspaper or news magazine, or tune into a news broadcast on radio or television. How does this information "travel," get written or photographed, and arrive in your home?

The profession and business of collecting and presenting information about current events is called journalism. The word "journalism" comes from the old French word *journal*, which meant "daily." Most journalism is a daily recording of events. We usually think of journalism today as including not only current news, but also feature articles on subjects of public interest and columns of opinions.

The basic form of journalism is news. Most large news publications and radio and TV broadcasting companies employ people to *cover* (go out and see) events as they are happening. Very often these people are assigned to cover specific places or topics, such as social events, local government meetings, or sports events. These *reporters* then report, or write about, what they have seen or heard. Since it is nearly impossible (and very expensive) to have a reporter at every spot in the world, many news publications rely on *news agencies* for much of their news. This is especially true of small-town newspapers. A news agency is a very large organization that employs reporters in many parts of the world. Newspapers pay these agencies for permission to print their news stories. The best-known news agencies in the United States are the Associated Press (AP) and United Press International

(UPI). The initials of these agencies appear on the top of their stories. How many articles that have come from news agencies can you find in your newspaper?

Another form of journalism is the *feature*. A feature article can be entertaining, informative, or instructive. Features include comic strips, cartoons, background articles on people and places in the news, art and theater reviews, and articles on cooking or gardening.

A third form of journalism is the expression of opinion. Opinions, or a writer's thoughts on a subject, appear in *editorials* (editor's essays), television and radio commentaries, *columns* (regularly published newspaper articles by one person), and letters to the editor. A good journalist keeps facts and opinions separate so that his or her audience can make up its own mind.

Journalists must decide which news is to be reported. They must also decide the manner in which stories will be presented. How important is a story? Should it be on the front page or at the beginning of the newscast? Will it get a big headline? In deciding these things, journalists play an important part in forming public opinion.

When people speak of journalists, they are usually thinking of reporters or writers. But many other people are involved in getting the news to you. Some of them are editors, photographers, and camera operators. The person in charge of the entire operation is called a *publisher* (for newspapers and magazines) or a *producer* (for broadcasting). Technicians are often not included in the journalism profession, although they are important to it. They include printers, distributers, broadcasting engineers, and dozens of other specialists.

Many young people go to college to study journalism. About 275 colleges and universities in the United States have schools and departments of jour-

nalism. To study journalism, students should have an aptitude for writing, photography, or art. They should have an interest in people and current events. They must be accurate in their writing and be curious about the world.

■ LEARN BY DOING

Would you like to be a journalist? You can put out a newspaper at home with some friends, or in school with your class. First, decide what kind of information you want to put in your "journal." Perhaps you would like to write about a class project. Did you take a trip that is worth reporting? Is there an interesting person in your community whom you could interview (ask questions)? You could include original stories, poems, riddles, and jokes, and announcements of forthcoming school events.

When you have put all the items you have written together, ask a parent or teacher to help you *publish* them. Your school probably has a machine on which you can make copies. You will find it exciting when you finally see your finished writing "in print." ■

ALSO READ: COMMUNICATION, MAGAZINE, NEWSPAPER, PUBLISHING, RADIO BROADCASTING, TELEVISION BROADCASTING.

▲ *Modern lightweight cameras and sound equipment have made news gathering much more streamlined. Journalists can relay news, complete with sound and videotapes, over thousands of miles in a matter of hours. And satellite communications can achieve this in seconds.*

There are about 1,600 daily newspapers in the United States, twice as many as in any other country.

▲ *Benito Juárez, Mexican political leader.*

▲ *The synagogue is the Jewish place of worship and learning. The word means "to bring together."*

JUÁREZ, BENITO (1806–1872)
Benito Juárez was one of the great Mexican patriots. He was born of Indian parents, and as a child knew the hardships suffered by the Indians of Mexico.

Juárez became governor of the state of Oaxaca at the age of 40. He was opposed to the harsh methods of the dictator of Mexico, General Santa Anna. He was forced to leave Mexico but returned to join in a revolution against the dictator.

In 1855, Santa Anna was defeated. Juárez tried to introduce a constitution that would bring new freedom to the poor. It took a three-year struggle, called the "War of Reform," before Juárez won. Juárez's new constitution took away most of the Roman Catholic Church's traditional powers and gave much of the Church's land to the poor. This displeased some powerful European nations, including France and Spain. French troops invaded the country. Maximilian, an Austrian archduke, was made Emperor of Mexico and Juárez fled again.

He set up his own capital in a town now named Juárez in his honor. Within three years, his brave resistance to the French brought about their defeat. He entered Mexico City in triumph and was made president in 1867. The foreign troops fled and Maximilian was executed. Juárez was reelected president in 1871. He had enormous popular support and died in office a national hero.

ALSO READ: MEXICO; HIDALGO Y COSTILLA, MIGUEL.

JUDAISM Judaism is one of the oldest religions in the world. The Old Testament, the first of the Bible, tells of a Hebrew tribal chief, Abraham, who lived in the Middle East about 4,000 years ago. Abraham was one of the first persons to believe in one God. The Bible tells how Abraham made a *covenant*, or agreement, promising to worship only God and to obey God's laws. In return, the descendants of Abraham would live in "a land of milk and honey," and prosper. God later gave the Ten Commandments to the Hebrew leader, Moses.

The early history and laws of Judaism are found in the *Torah*, the first five books of the Old Testament. The *Talmud*, another collection of ancient writings, includes laws governing everyday life and interpretations of these laws. Both the Talmud and the Torah contain all the beliefs and rules that not only bound the Jewish people together through centuries of wandering, but also form the religious and political laws of the Jewish people wherever they live. They include ideas about the equality of all members of a community, personal liberty and love of freedom, personal morality, property rights, and the rights of all human beings, in addition to the belief in one God who is creator, lawgiver, and king.

Judaism teaches that people must be fair and kind to others. A person is supposed to live a good life simply for the satisfaction of being a good human being, without any promise of a reward. Many Jews believe that a leader, called the *Messiah*, will someday come to save all people. Each Jewish community, or congregation, is led by a *rabbi*, a religious teacher and scholar. Many Jews worship and study in a special building, called a *synagogue*. A *cantor* sings the prayers when the congregation worships.

Certain days are special to the Jews. One is the *Sabbath*, a day of prayer. It begins at sunset on Friday evening and ends at sunset, Saturday evening. (All days in the Hebrew calendar are figured from sundown to sundown.) *Yom Kippur*, the Day of Atonement, is the holiest day of the year, on which Jews fast and pray. *Rosh Hashanah* is the Jewish New Year.

Judaism has laws governing much of daily life. There are laws (called *kosher* laws) about the preparation of food and what may or may not be eaten. Weddings and funerals are performed as commanded in the Torah and Talmud. All Jewish boys are circumcised on the eighth day after birth. At the age of 13, boys officially become adults in a special ceremony, called a *bar mitzvah*. A similar ceremony, a *bat mitzvah*, is for girls.

Three main branches of Judaism exist today. People who carefully follow all the ancient traditions and laws are called Orthodox Jews. People less strict in their observance are called Conservative Jews. Reform Jews do not always observe traditional laws, but they believe in the ideals of Judaism. Approximately 17 million Jews are scattered throughout the world today. Most of them live in the United States, the Soviet Union, Canada, and Israel.

ALSO READ: BIBLE, CHRISTIANITY, DEAD SEA SCROLLS, HANUKKAH, ISLAM, ISRAEL, JERUSALEM, JEWISH HISTORY, NEW YEAR'S DAY, PASSOVER, YOM KIPPUR.

JUDO One of the few sports that began as a method of self-defense is judo, a system of fighting without weapons. (The word "judo" means "the gentle way" in Japanese.) Judo was developed in 1882 by Dr. Jigoro Kano of Japan, who based it on *jujitsu*, an ancient system of hand-to-hand fighting. Today, all Japanese students receive training in judo. The sport has also become popular in other countries, including the United States.

A judo fighter wears a loose-fitting white jacket and trousers. The color of the belt he or she wears indicates the amount of skill achieved. A beginner wears a white one. The most skillful wear black belts. Fighters may compete in either *randori* (free

combat or competition) or *kata* (planned practice of the various movements).

Judo experts can overcome larger, stronger persons. They can do this because judo depends on concentration and the use of balance and leverage rather than on size. Players use nonresistance to get their opponents off balance. They do not fight back when they are attacked. In this way, their opponents are thrown off balance by the force of their own attack. (You have the same sort of experience if you push hard on a door that opens easily. Your own strength can make you trip or fall.) The nonresisting players can then overcome their opponents.

A judo competitor uses two kinds of techniques to overpower an opponent. The first group of techniques offers him or her several ways to throw the opponent's body. The throws are named for the part of the body involved—hand, foot, back, side, hips, shoulders, and so on. The second group concerns *locks*, or ways to keep an opponent's body from moving. Locks are applied to the legs, arms, or neck.

Do not try to learn judo by yourself or with a friend. Most cities and towns have judo clubs where beginners can learn safely and carefully with qualified instructors.

ALSO READ: EXERCISE, GYMNASTICS, KARATE, PHYSICAL EDUCATION.

JUGGLING One of the most spectacular acts in show business is that of the skilled juggler. Professional jugglers appear in stage shows and on television. The most skilled jugglers can keep ten or more objects in motion at the same time.

Balancing acts are also part of juggling. A good juggler can balance a long pole on his or her nose. On top of the pole is a balanced plate, which is spinning rapidly around and around.

▲ *A Jewish boy formally takes on the religious duties of an adult in a ceremony called a* bar mitzvah.

▼ *A judo contest is between 5 and 20 minutes long and is a test of skill rather than endurance.*

DATES OF SPECIAL EVENTS IN JULY

1 • First circulating library was opened in Philadelphia (1731).
   • Battle of Gettysburg began (1863).
   • Battle of the Somme began during World War I. It is the bloodiest battle of recorded history (1916).
   • Dominion Day, a national holiday in Canada.
2 • President James Garfield was shot. He died September 19 (1881).
3 • Samuel de Champlain founded Quebec (1608).
4 • Independence Day to celebrate the adoption of the Declaration of Independence by the Continental Congress in 1776.
   • First rodeo competition (1888).
5 • Venezuela became the first South American country to gain independence from Spain (1811).
   • Twenty-sixth Amendment to the Constitution, setting the voting age at 18, was proclaimed (1971).
6 • John Paul Jones, an American hero of the seas, was born (1747).
7 • First American is made a saint: Frances Xavier Cabrini (1946).
11 • Robert Bruce, Scottish patriot who freed Scotland from English rule, was born (1274).
   • President John Quincy Adams was born (1767).
   • United States Marine Corps was founded (1798).
   • Alexander Hamilton was killed in a duel with Aaron Burr (1804).
12 • Henry David Thoreau, American author, was born (1817).
   • Orange Day in Northern Ireland (Ulster). Protestants celebrate victory over the Catholics in the Battle of the Boyne in 1690.
13 • "Live Aid," an all-day rock music concert held in Philadelphia and London in aid of Ethiopian famine victims, was broadcast around the world to 152 countries and roughly one third of the world's population (1985).
14 • Storming of the Bastille, a Paris prison, touched off the French Revolution (1789).
15 • Rembrandt, Dutch painter and etcher, was born (1606).
16 • District of Columbia was established (1790).
   • First atomic bomb was exploded at Alamogordo, New Mexico (1945).
17 • Spain officially gave up Florida to the United States (1821).
   • Spanish Civil War began (1936).
18 • Disneyland, then the world's largest amusement resort, was opened in Anaheim, California (1955).
19 • First meeting organized in United States to press for women's rights took place in New York (1848).
20 • First manned landing on the moon (1969).
21 • Ernest Hemingway, American author, was born (1899).
22 • Battle of Atlanta took place during the Civil War (1864).
24 • Simon Bolivar, Venezuelan freedom fighter, was born (1783).
25 • George Stephenson first demonstrated a successful steam locomotive (1814).
26 • George Bernard Shaw, Irish playwright, was born (1856).
27 • Korean War ended (1953).
   • United States State Department was formed (1789).
29 • Benito Mussolini, Italian dictator, was born (1883).
   • Prince Charles, heir to the British throne, and Lady Diana Spencer were married in St. Paul's Cathedral, London (1981).
30 • English attacked the Spanish Armada, defeating Spain (1588).
   • First representative assembly in American colonies met in Jamestown, Virginia (1619).

At the same time, the juggler may use both hands to juggle balls, hoops, tenpins, or plates.

■ **LEARN BY DOING**

For juggling, you need lots of practice and good coordination between your eyes and your hands. The simplest form of juggling is with two round objects—for example, two oranges or two small balls of the same size. Holding a ball in each hand, toss the right-hand ball into the air slightly to the left. At the same time, quickly toss the other ball from your left hand across to your right hand. As soon as the ball is released from the left hand, the hand should be ready to catch the other ball. Continue to toss and catch the two balls, trying to develop a constant rhythm in your juggling. When you're ready, try the same movements with three balls. ■

ALSO READ: ACROBATICS, CIRCUS.

JULY July is a popular time for vacations. It is one of the best months for swimming, camping, and hiking. July can be a very hot month in the northern part of the world. Flowers and crops grow in the warm sunshine. But in the southern half of the world (below the equator), July is the middle of winter.

Independence Day, or the Fourth of July, is an American holiday. On July 4, 1776, the Declaration of Independence was announced by the members of the Continental Con-

▼ *July's flower is the water lily.*

gress. Most people do not have to work on this holiday. Celebrations are held with parades, speeches, and fireworks.

July is the seventh month of the year and has 31 days. In the old Roman calendar, July had about 36 days and was called *Quintilis*, meaning "fifth" in Latin. Julius Caesar ordered the Roman calendar to be changed, and Quintilis became the seventh month. After the calendar was changed, the month was still called Quintilis for a while. Many people believe that Julius Caesar renamed the month after himself.

July's flower is the water lily or larkspur. Its birthstone is the ruby.

ALSO READ: CALENDAR, HOLIDAY, INDEPENDENCE DAY, MONTH, SEASON, SUMMER.

JUNE "And what is so rare as a day in June?" These words, written by the American poet, James Russell Lowell, express the way many people feel about June. For many children, June is the month when school ends and summer vacation begins.

In the northern part of the world, the first day of summer (the summer solstice) falls on June 21 or 22. It is the longest day of the year. The weather is warm, and flowers, trees, and shrubs are in bloom. But in the southern part of the world (below the equator), winter begins during this month.

June is the sixth month of the year. It has 30 days. In the old Roman calendar, it was the fourth month, and it had only 29 days. The extra day was added when Julius Caesar had the calendar changed. June's flower is the rose. The birthstone for June is pearl or alexandrite. Father's Day is celebrated on the third Sunday of June.

No one knows for sure where the name June comes from. It might have been named for Juno, the Roman goddess of marriage. June is still a

DATES OF SPECIAL EVENTS IN JUNE

3 • Jefferson Davis, president of the Confederacy during the Civil War, was born (1808).
5 • First public balloon flight took place in France (1783).
6 • Nathan Hale, American patriot, was born (1755).
 • YMCA (Young Men's Christian Association) organized in London (1844).
 • D-Day, the invasion of Europe by Allied troops. They landed on the coast of Normandy in the heart of German-occupied territory (1944).
8 • Frank Lloyd Wright, American architect, was born (1869).
9 • Peter the Great, Czar of Russia, was born (1672).
 • George Stephenson, known as the inventor of the railroads, was born (1781).
 • Cole Porter, American writer of songs popular the world over, was born (1893).
11 • John Constable, English painter famous for his beautiful landscapes, was born (1776).
 • Continental Congress appointed a committee to draw up a declaration of independence (1776).
14 • Continental Congress adopted the U.S. flag (1777).
 • Harriet Beecher Stowe, author of *Uncle Tom's Cabin*, was born (1811).
 • First nonstop flight across the Atlantic Ocean, from Newfoundland to Ireland, made by Alcock and Brown (1919).
15 • King John of England signed Magna Carta (1215).
 • George Washington was made Commander in Chief of the Continental Army (1775).
 • Edvard Grieg, Norwegian composer, was born (1843).
16 • Ford Motor Company was founded (1903).
17 • Mississippi River was discovered by Father Jacques Marquette and Louis Joliet (1673).
 • Battle of Bunker Hill, first big battle of the American Revolution (1775).
18 • United States declared war on Britain (1812).
 • Battle of Waterloo in which Napoleon was defeated (1815).
20 • Congress adopted the design for the Great Seal of the United States (1782).
 • Queen Victoria of England was crowned (1837).
 • President Andrew Johnson announced the purchase of Alaska from Russia (1867).
21 • U.S. forces captured Okinawa from Japan after one of the bloodiest battles of World War II in the Pacific (1945).
22 • France surrendered to Germany (1940).
23 • William Penn signed famous treaty with Indians (1683).
25 • George Custer and his troops were killed by the Sioux Indians at the Little Big Horn in Montana (1876).
 • North Korea attacked South Korea, beginning the Korean War (1950).
26 • United Nations Charter signed by 50 nations in San Francisco (1945).
 • Pearl S. Buck, American Nobel prize-winning novelist, was born (1892).
27 • Helen Keller, deaf and blind American who grew up to be an author and lecturer, was born (1880).
28 • Archduke Franz Ferdinand of Austria was assassinated. His death was used as an excuse to start World War I (1914).
 • Treaty of Versailles was signed, officially ending World War I (1919).

▲ *June's flower is the rose.*

▲ *Carl Jung's theories about the workings of the human mind have greatly influenced modern treatment of mental illness.*

popular month for weddings. It may have been named after an important Roman family, Junius. The month of June was originally dedicated to youth, so it may have come from the Latin word *juniores*, which means "young people."

ALSO READ: CALENDAR, MONTH, SEASON, SUMMER.

JUNG, CARL (1875–1961) The young Carl Gustav Jung, son of a Swiss clergyman, planned to become an archeologist, but his interest turned to medicine. He became fascinated by psychology (the study of the mind). Jung was especially interested in *psychoanalysis*, the system of examining the mind worked out by Sigmund Freud. Freud used this method in treating diseases of the mind. Jung later developed his own theory, called *analytical psychology*.

Jung's ideas about what governs human behavior emphasized the development of the human race from its primitive beginnings. His work prompted the study of primitive peoples and their mythology to help understand the human personality. Jung suggested that we all share some unconscious memories of the experiences of our early ancestors. This is why some of the same ideas are found in different cultures all over the world.

Jung also invented the terms *extrovert* (outward-looking; interested in others), and *introvert* (thoughtful and inward-looking) to describe types of personalities.

ALSO READ: FREUD, SIGMUND; PSYCHOLOGY.

JUNGLE A jungle is a forest that grows in a hot, wet climate near the equator. Jungles are different from the forests of temperate (medium-temperature) climates. Often called *rain forests*, jungles can grow up only in areas that get over 80 inches (200 cm) of rain a year and have an average temperature of about 80°F (27°C). Most jungles have wet and dry seasons but they are hot all year round. A jungle is a thick, tangled growth of trees, vines, and grasses. Vines and creepers wind around the trees, which are often covered with parasitic plants and animals. People cannot walk through a jungle without cutting their way through the undergrowth.

Jungles are found in South America, Central America, Africa, Southeast Asia, India, Australia, and on other islands in the South Pacific. The kinds of plant and animals that live in a jungle depend on its location. Plants in Asian jungles are completely different from those in African and South American jungles. Many plants that never get very large in temperate climates grow to giant sizes in the jungle.

A jungle contains at least three distinct levels of plant and animal life. Each level is an *ecosystem*—a group of plants and animals that live with and feed off each other. The animals of one level may never see or have anything to do with animals on the other levels.

The first level starts on the ground and goes up to about 25 feet (8 m). Short palm trees, ferns, and many beautiful plants, such as the philodendron, which people enjoy as houseplants in colder places, grow on this level. Most of the large jungle mammals are also found on the jungle floor. Tapirs, anteaters, jaguars, and wild pigs live in South American jungles. Tigers and leopards live in Asian and African jungles. Some kinds of birds—and the insects they live on—live at ground level. Crocodiles live in jungle rivers. Hippopotamuses make their homes near the rivers in jungles. Giant butterflies and moths also live on the first level. Many kinds of snakes—some of them poisonous—live here. Even certain crabs that normally live only near water can exist on the damp jungle ground.

The second level covers the area from 25 to 50 feet (8 to 15 m) above the ground. The animals that live in the tops of the taller trees can be found here. The pottos of African jungles and other small mammals live on this level. The tadpoles of tree frogs swim in puddles of water held up by giant leaves. These tadpoles become frogs, but they never go down to the ground. They gobble up insects that live on this level. The plant life here includes giant ferns, mosses, and pink, red, and purple orchids, which cling to the branches of trees.

The top level of the jungle is called the *canopy*. This area includes the tops of the very tallest trees, 100 feet (30 m) high or more. Vines and the foliage at the tops of trees meet and intertwine here, forming a kind of roof over the jungle. Many kinds of monkeys live here. They travel along—and swing from—branches and vines. In South American jungles, the sloth spends its whole life hanging from high branches. Its fur looks green because of the algae (tiny plants) that grow in it. At the top of the canopy—in the sunlight—are the huge, brightly colored flowers and fruits of trees and vines whose roots are planted in the ground 100 feet (30 m) below. Butterflies, bees, grasshoppers, other insects, parrots (and hummingbirds, in South America) flit back and forth in the canopy.

Many well-known and widely used products come from jungles. The rattan palm and bamboo of Asia are used to make porch furniture. Teak trees grow in Asian jungles, and mahogany trees grow in Central and South America. Both trees furnish wood prized by furniture makers. The chicle tree, from which chewing gum is made, grows in Central America. Balsa trees, used to make model airplanes, boats, and buoys, grow in American jungles.

People of the Jungle The jungle is a very hot and steamy place for people to live. Much of a person's energy is used up surviving the high temperature and the humidity. Little sun reaches the dark jungle floor, so farming is impossible unless a clearing is made. The few people who live in the jungle live in small villages in the clearings or at the edge of the jungle. The people hunt, fish, and gather fruit. They build houses out of bamboo, wood, and leaves from the jungle. They make rafts, weapons, and tools from bamboo and other jungle materials.

Other Tropical Forests *Seasonal forests* grow up each year in areas that

▲ *Jungle vegetation covers vast areas of India. In these areas, rivers are often the only means of transportation.*

By far the noisiest animals of the South American jungle are the howler monkeys. It is said that if the wind is in the right direction you can hear them howling for a distance of more than 4 miles (7 km).

◄ *Tropical jungles are usually dense forests of high trees. People in these regions must clear plots of land for cultivation.*

CANOPY LAYER
100 ft. (30 m)

MIDDLE LAYER
25–50 ft. (8–15 m)

LOWER LAYER
0–25 ft. (8 m)

▲ *The three main layers of a rain forest:*

Canopy layer: *A thick mass of treetops. Many birds and animals live here.*

Middle layer: *Lianas (creepers) and climbing plants struggle toward the light.*

Lower layer: *Many animals, shrubs and young trees. Dark.*

have a rainy season followed by an extremely dry season. During the dry season, leaves fall and ferns die. Then the rain falls and everything sprouts again or becomes green.

Cloud forests grow on tropical mountainsides. They are called "cloud forests" because they are always misty and rainy. Mosses and lichens grow over all the other plants. In some places they form a layer thicker than the tree trunks.

Tropical rain forests are "grown-up" jungles. Over long periods of time, the canopy of a jungle becomes so thick that it blocks all the sunlight from the plants and animals living below. Many plants on the lower levels then die. Because of the darkness, the trunks of the tall trees have no leaves. Therefore, there is much less undergrowth in a tropical rain forest than in other jungles.

ALSO READ: ALGAE, ANIMAL, CLIMATE, LICHEN, MAMMAL, MONKEY, MOSSES AND LIVERWORTS, ORCHID, PALM, PLANT.

JUVENILE DELINQUENCY

Continual lawbreaking or antisocial behavior by a boy or girl under a certain legal age—usually 18—is called juvenile delinquency. It may include such acts as using harmful drugs, stealing, destroying property, hurting others, or drinking alcoholic beverages. A *juvenile delinquent* is a young person whose behavior goes against the set *norms* (patterns) of society. The manner in which juvenile delinquency is treated by a community may decide if a young person turns toward or away from an adult life of crime.

What makes young persons break laws? Often they feel anger toward the adult world. Their parents may be divorced or separated. Or the parents may fight often, may not love them, or may not discipline them. If the parents do not show respect for the

community and its laws, the young persons may not either.

Poverty may also cause youths to break laws. They may begin to steal things that others have but that they cannot afford. If they live in a slum, they may hate the run-down houses and poor schools there and may destroy property out of anger.

When there are no activities for young people in a community, they are more likely to get into trouble. Bored teenagers may roam the neighborhoods in gangs, breaking windows or stealing cars. Young people may also commit crimes just to be accepted by other young people who do these things.

What happens to young persons who break laws? Sometimes the police talk to the youths' parents or send them to an agency for help. Often, however, the young persons must go to juvenile court. The court may send them to a *probation officer*, a person who will try to help the youths solve their problems, and will check on them to make sure they stay out of trouble. The court can also send the delinquent to a *psychiatrist*, a doctor who helps people who have mental or emotional problems. If youths live in unhappy families, the court may place them in *foster homes* with *foster parents*, who try to give these young people happy homes. Sometimes, juvenile delinquents are sent to live in state institutions. In recent years, more experimental approaches in the treatment of young offenders have included group therapy, challenging work experiences, and individual counseling.

Young people who become juvenile delinquents often hurt themselves more than their communities. Their offenses sometimes keep them from going to school and getting good jobs. They lose self-respect, and the respect of others.

ALSO READ: ADOLESCENCE, CRIME, DRUG ABUSE, DRUGS, NARCOTICS, PSYCHOLOGY, SOCIAL WORK, SOCIOLOGY.

KAMEHAMEHA I (1758–1819)

The first king of all the Hawaiian Islands was Kamehameha. At first, Kamehameha ruled only one "big island" of Hawaii. He wanted to rule all five of the major Hawaiian Islands. In 1795, he gathered an army of about 16,000 warriors, bought guns from white traders, and brought together enough war canoes to line the beach for 4 miles (6 km).

His invasion force conquered the island of Maui and then attacked the second largest island, Oahu (where Honolulu is today). The climax of the bloody battle came high in the central mountains. Legend says that several hundred defenders were driven off the high cliffs to their death. Kamehameha later gained control of the two remaining islands, unifying all Hawaii into one kingdom in 1810.

King Kamehameha encouraged trade. Hawaiian traders sold sandalwood to ship captains who sold it in China to make incense and fine furniture. Kamehameha encouraged fishing, farming, and industry. He some-

times caught his own fish, built boats, and farmed a small vegetable patch. But he kept a stern hand on warlords to keep his kingdom unified.

ALSO READ: HAWAII.

KAMPUCHEA (Cambodia)

This Southeast Asian country has been officially renamed Cambodia. It is a Communist republic, about the size of Missouri. (See the map with the article on ASIA.)

The heart of Cambodia is a large fertile plain drained by the Mekong River and its tributaries. The country is bordered by low mountains that are covered with tropical forests. The climate is ideal for growing rice, the chief crop. Corn, tobacco, cotton, rubber, and sugar are also cultivated. Many people live in villages along rivers and lakes and work in nearby rice paddies.

Cambodia's climate is controlled by the *monsoons* (seasonal winds). During the summer monsoon from May to October, heavy rains fall,

▲ *A bronze statue of Kamehameha I stands before the Judiciary building in Honolulu's civic center. Thousands of flowers are draped around the statue every June 11, Kamehameha Day.*

KAMPUCHEA (CAMBODIA)

Capital City: Phnom Penh (300,000 people).
Area: 69,898 square miles (181,022 sq. km).
Population: 6,800,000.
Government: Communist republic.
Natural Resources: Phosphate, iron ore.
Export Products: Rice, rubber.
Unit of Money: Riel.
Official Language: Khmer.

▲ *Angkor Wat in Kampuchea is a great temple built by the Khmer people in the early 1100's.*

causing the Mekong River to swell and back up into the large Tônlé Sap ("Great Lake"), which then increases threefold in size. The houses here are built on stilts. Fishermen live on rafts so that their homes can float when the water rises. Cambodia's rivers and lakes are used as waterways to move goods and people from one place to another.

The capital city, Phnom Penh, has a beautiful royal palace, tree-lined streets, and a bustling river marketplace. Large numbers of Chinese and Vietnamese shopkeepers live in Phnom Penh. Textile factories and sawmills manufacture goods that are shipped to many parts of the world. Phnom Penh is Cambodia's only truly large city. Medium-sized and small cities stand on the plains.

The powerful Khmer empire was centered in Cambodia from the 800's to the 1300's. The most important ancient capital was Angkor Wat. It was deserted after the Thais conquered the Khmers. Magnificent ruins of the temples and palaces built by Khmer kings still stand in the forest. The people still speak Khmer and follow the religion of Buddhism. Cambodia became a French protectorate in the 1800's. It became independent in 1953. Cambodia tried to be neutral in the struggle between Communists and non-Communists in neighboring Vietnam. In 1970, a coup toppled the monarchy and Cambodia became officially the Khmer

Republic. It fought a five-year war against Communist takeover, receiving help from the United States and South Vietnam. However, in 1975, the Communist Khmer Rouge forces finally won control and set up a new government. The country's borders were closed.

The Khmer Rouge renamed the country Democratic Kampuchea. About a million people were killed by the Khmer Rouge and others died of starvation and disease. In 1979, Vietnamese and Kampuchean troops overthrew the Khmer Rouge government. However, fighting with Khmer Rouge guerrillas, who had fled into the forests, continued in the 1980's.

ALSO READ: ASIA, VIETNAM, VIETNAM WAR.

KANGAROO Kangaroos live only in Australia, Tasmania, and New Guinea. They are the Australian national animal. Kangaroos come in all sizes. The largest kangaroo is the red kangaroo, which is sometimes 7 feet (2 m) tall and weighs 200 pounds (90 kg). The smallest is the rat kangaroo, which is about the size of a rabbit. Medium-size kangaroos are also called *wallabies*. Another kind of kangaroo is the tree kangaroo. It has strong claws that help it hold on to branches as it jumps from tree to tree. It even sleeps in trees.

The red kangaroo is a shy, nervous

animal that eats grass and leaves. If a kangaroo sees a wild dog or another enemy approaching, it hops away on its giant hind legs. A red kangaroo usually hops 5 to 10 feet (1.5 to 3 m) in a single jump. The red kangaroo can travel 25 miles (40 km) an hour. A kangaroo will defend itself by kicking with its powerful hind legs, which can kill another animal.

Kangaroos belong to a branch of the animal kingdom called the *marsupials*. Each female marsupial has a pouch, or furry pocket, under the skin of its belly. A female kangaroo usually has only one baby at a time. The newborn kangaroo is only about an inch (2.5 cm) long. As soon as the baby is born, it makes its way to its mother's pouch. Inside the mother's pouch is a nipple. Milk comes from the end of the nipple. The newborn kangaroo fastens its mouth to the nipple. It lies cozily in its mother's pouch for about two months, while it develops enough to begin to explore the outside world.

A young kangaroo is called a "joey." The joey learns to eat grass and take care of itself. But the joey hurries back to its mother's pouch whenever there is danger about.

ALSO READ: ANIMAL KINGDOM, AUSTRALIAN MAMMALS, MAMMAL, MARSUPIAL.

KANSAS You have probably watched gunfights in the dusty streets of Dodge City—in movies or on television. Have you ever wondered where Dodge City is? It is in southwestern Kansas. The town was founded in 1872 on the Arkansas River near Fort Dodge. Railroads reached it three years later, and Dodge City became a cattle town.

History was made in Kansas, largely because the state lies at the nation's crossroads. It is at the very center of the 48 states that make up the main part of the United States.

Long wagon trains traveling west passed through Kansas on the Santa Fe and Oregon trails. Some of the old forts, which were built along the wagon trails to protect travelers from Indian attacks, can still be seen.

The Land Kansas is almost a perfect rectangle. Only the northeast corner of the boundary line is crooked. The Missouri River forms the boundary there. Nebraska is north of Kansas, and Oklahoma is south of it. Colorado lies to the west, and Missouri to the east.

Nature has divided Kansas into two very different parts—western Kansas and eastern Kansas. The two areas differ in surface, soil, and climate, and have different kinds of agriculture.

Western Kansas is the Great Plains. The land is highest near the Colorado border, and it slopes toward the east. Most of the land has gentle hills, but some of the slopes are very steep. In places, flat-topped hills with rocky sides rise above the plain. Much of the soil is sandy, but all of it is fertile and good for farming. Rainfall is light in western Kansas, too light for raising corn. Short buffalo grass grows wild here. The bison that once roamed the plains fed on it, and so do cattle today. Certain kinds of wheat need only light rainfall. The chief crop of western Kansas is winter wheat. It is planted in October and harvested in late spring.

Eastern Kansas is prairie land.

▲ *Kangaroos, like other marsupials, produce their young at an early stage of development. The young crawl into their mothers' pouches, where they continue to develop in safety.*

▼ *Boot Hill Cemetery in Dodge City, the resting place of outlaws who died in the violent days of the old West.*

NEBRASKA   MISSOURI

KANSAS

Capital
Topeka (119,000 people)

Area
82,264 square miles
(213,047 sq. km)
Rank: 14th

Population
2,495,000 people
Rank: 32nd

Statehood
January 29, 1861
(34th state admitted)

Principal rivers
Kansas, or Kaw, River
Arkansas River

Highest point
4,135 feet (1,260 m), on
the Colorado border

Largest city
Wichita (283,000 people)

Motto
Ad Astra per Aspera (To
the stars through
difficulties)

Song
"Home on the Range"

Famous people
Thomas Hart Benton,
Amelia Earhart, Dwight
D. Eisenhower, Carry
Nation, William Allen
White

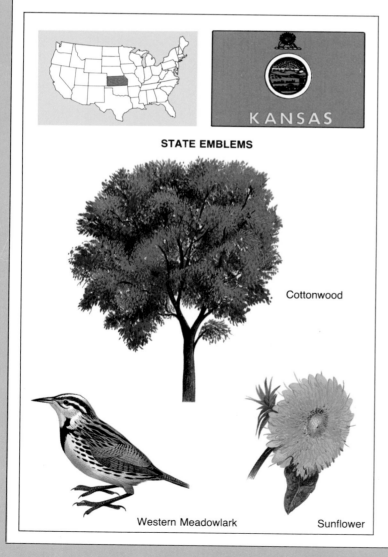

KANSAS

STATE EMBLEMS

Cottonwood

Western Meadowlark   Sunflower

▼ *The busy railroad
yards in Kansas City.*

Rain is much more plentiful here. Tall grass once covered the fertile valleys. Its long roots, decaying year after year, made the soil richer and richer. Good rainfall, fertile soil, and hot summers are just right for corn. It is the main crop of eastern Kansas. Before the land of eastern Kansas was planted with corn, the prairie was covered with tall, waving grass. This prairie grass can be seen in the area called the Flint Hills, an upland section that stretches from north to south.

History The story of Kansas begins with the four main Indian tribes—the Pawnee, the Osage, the Wichita, and the Kaw. The Kaw Indians were also called the Kansas, which means "people of the south wind." The state got its name from them.

The Indians lived in villages of earthen huts. They raised corn, beans, and squash, and went out in bands to hunt buffalo (bison). They hunted on foot, because Indians had no horses until the Spanish came.

Spaniards were the first Europeans to come to this region. A small army from New Spain (Mexico) arrived in 1541. Its commander was a nobleman named Francisco Coronado. He was looking for a land rich in gold and silver. French explorers claimed the region in the late 1600's, but very few settlers went there during the next 100 years.

Spaniards had started ranches in New Mexico. Indians found that ranch horses were easy to steal, and some horses simply wandered away from the ranches. Herds of wild horses roamed the Great Plains. Indians all the way to Kansas—and beyond—soon had their own herds.

The United States bought France's large territory of Louisiana in 1803. All of what is now Kansas, except the southwestern corner, was part of that Louisiana Purchase. Americans began exploring the new territory.

The first new settlers in Kansas

were Indians from farther east. The U.S. government moved them there from their eastern lands to make room for white farmers. Many of the Indian newcomers were farmers themselves. They cleared land and built cabins in eastern Kansas.

More white settlers began to move to Kansas after Congress passed the Kansas-Nebraska Act in 1854. This law created the territories of Kansas and Nebraska. Americans at this time were quarreling over whether to allow slavery in new states and territories. The Kansas-Nebraska Act permitted the people of the Kansas and Nebraska territories to decide the issue for themselves. Northerners and Southerners both came to live in Kansas. The Southerners wanted to use slave labor on their farms. The Northerners wanted to keep slavery out of Kansas. Many violent battles were fought. John Brown, the famous anti-slavery leader, led a raid at Pottowatomie Creek in 1856, killing five pro-slavery men. The Northerners of Kansas finally became stronger in numbers, so they had their way. Kansas entered the Union as a free, non-slave state in 1861. The Civil War began that same year, and fighting again broke out in what was called "Bleeding Kansas."

New railroads brought thousands of settlers to Kansas during the late 1860's and the 1870's. Many freed slaves and Union veterans of the Civil War were among the new settlers.

▲ *The state capitol in Topeka, the capital of Kansas since 1861.*

In 1855 there were fewer than 9,000 people in the whole of Kansas. Five years later the population had increased to 107,000.

1355

The geographical center of the 48 states lies in Smith County, Kansas, 2 miles (3 km) to the northwest of Lebanon. Just 42 miles (68 km) to the south, in Osborne County, is a point from which all surveys of the North American Continent are measured. This is called the geodetic center of North America.

▲ *Karate fighters focus the muscle power of their entire body into one blow of great force. Hands, fists, elbows, and feet are all used to deliver karate blows.*

The Mennonites, a religious group from Russia, settled in western Kansas in 1874. These people brought wheat seed to plant. The wheat, called Turkey Red, was a kind that needed only a little rain. The Mennonites started the wheat farming that now brings much wealth to Kansas.

Kansans At Work Manufacturing earns more money than agriculture does in Kansas today. Most factories are in the three largest cities, Wichita, Kansas City, and Topeka. Aircraft, motor vehicles, and other transportation equipment are the state's leading manufactured products. Food products and chemicals are next in manufacturing importance.

Agriculture is not far behind manufacturing in money value. Kansas produces more than a billion dollars' worth of livestock a year. Wheat is the most valuable crop. Kansas leads the entire United States in wheat production. Three other grains—sorghum, corn, and hay—are also important crops. Much grain is fed to cattle, hogs, and sheep instead of being sold.

Kansas has resources under its soil, too. Petroleum brings the most money. Natural gas is next.

ALSO READ: BROWN, JOHN; CORONADO, FRANCISCO; EARP, WYATT; GREAT PLAINS; HICKOK, WILD BILL; LOUISIANA PURCHASE; PRAIRIE; WESTWARD MOVEMENT.

KARATE Karate is an Oriental method of hand-to-hand combat. It was first practiced about two thousand years ago in India, China, and Korea. The fighting techniques of karate were developed further by the Japanese after the 1600's. Many U.S. soldiers learned karate in World War II, the Korean War, and the Vietnam War. An expert in karate can split a brick or board in two with one blow of the hand or foot. The word "karate" means "empty fist" in Japanese.

In karate, fighters use their hands, elbows, knees, feet, and heads to strike blows to vital points, such as the stomachs or throats, of their opponents' bodies. Since karate experts can kill with a single blow, they will only use it as a form of self-defense. Today, karate is a sport, requiring intense training and discipline. Students trained in karate are taught to avoid striking their opponents. Contests are usually judged according to the skill shown in the movements.

There are various levels of achievement and skill in karate. The students must earn the right to advance. As their technique improves, the students' instructor awards them different colored belts. Karate clothing consists of loose-fitting, white trousers and a jacket without buttons. A belt is worn around the outside of the jacket. Usually, the beginners wear a white belt. As they progress, they will successively wear a purple, then a brown belt. If they become skillful enough, they will earn the right to wear a black belt.

Karate should never be attempted without an instructor. Before the karate students match their skill against an opponent, they must spend many hours in training and conditioning. The important requirements of karate training are balance, coordination, breath control, and timing.

ALSO READ: EXERCISE, JUDO.

KEATS, JOHN (1795–1821) One of the greatest poets in English was John Keats. You may have heard the poem that begins:

"Season of mists and mellow fruitfulness,
Close bosom friend of the maturing sun;"

These lines by Keats come from a poem called *Ode to Autumn*. Other odes (short poems) by Keats include *On a Grecian Urn* and *To a Nightingale*.

Keats wrote these poems when he was in his early 20's. He was born in London, England, and both his parents died before he was 15. He became apprenticed to a surgeon, and was training to become a doctor when he realized that poetry was the most important thing in his life.

His first book of poems was published in 1817, but few people read it. However, among those who did recognize Keats's talent were some leading writers of the time, including Leigh Hunt and Percy Bysshe Shelley. They befriended Keats and encouraged him to write more.

Keats loved the world of nature and also the world of myth and legend. Many of his best poems capture a moment of beauty, immortalizing it in verse before it vanished with the passing of time. Keats wrote:

"A thing of beauty is joy for ever;
Its loveliness increases; it will never
    pass into nothingness. . ."

Keats's own life was short. In 1818 he showed signs of tuberculosis, a disease for which there was no cure at that time. He went to Italy, hoping the warmer climate would restore his health. But the illness worsened, and he died in Rome, in 1821.

ALSO READ: POETRY; SHELLEY, PERCY AND MARY.

KELLER, HELEN (1880–1968)

A baby girl born in Tuscumbia, Alabama, was a normal, healthy, happy baby until she was 18 months old. Then she became very sick. Her illness left her both blind and deaf. Soon she forgot all the sights and sounds of her babyhood and the few words she had learned.

She was examined by many doctors, but there seemed no hope that the girl, Helen Adams Keller, would ever be able to understand or communicate with others. When she was nearly seven, Helen's parents asked the Perkins Institute for the Blind and Deaf in Boston to send a teacher to help the child. Anne Sullivan, a young teacher, came to the Keller home to help Helen.

Anne Sullivan became Helen's constant companion and began to teach her about the world that Helen could not see or hear. Miss Sullivan used the manual alphabet to "spell" the names of objects that Helen could feel with her fingers. Miss Sullivan would place her fingers in Helen's palm and spell the name of an object by changing the position of her fingers. The first word Helen learned was *water*. Over and over again Miss Sullivan would spill water over Helen's hand and then spell the word for water. One day Helen suddenly got the idea—the movement of fingers in her hand meant the same thing as the wet "stuff" that she felt. For the first time, Helen realized she could communicate with someone.

Helen began to learn rapidly. Within two years, she had learned to read and write well in Braille, the method used by blind people. Later, she learned to speak by putting her fingers against Miss Sullivan's throat and feeling the vibrations of Miss Sullivan's speech. Helen would then put her fingers against her own throat and try to make the same kinds of vibrations. Miss Sullivan taught Helen the subjects that other children study in school and prepared her for college. Helen graduated with honors from Radcliffe College, where for four years Miss Sullivan "spelled" all the lectures into her hand.

Helen Keller devoted the rest of her long life to helping the blind and the deaf. She and Miss Sullivan traveled throughout the world, making appearances to raise money for this cause. After Miss Sullivan's death, Polly Thompson became Miss Keller's companion. Helen Keller wrote many articles and books to help people understand their responsibilities toward the handicapped. She was active in her work until her death.

▲ *A drawing of John Keats at the age of 21 by the artist Benjamin Haydon.*

▲ *Helen Keller, American author and social worker, blind and deaf from the age of two.*

▲ *President John F. Kennedy receives a traditional ticker-tape welcome from the people of New York City. His term of office ended abruptly with his assassination in November 1963.*

■ **LEARN BY DOING**

When you have finished reading this sentence, shut your eyes tightly, hold your hands firmly over your ears, and think what it would be like if your world were totally dark and without sound—all the time. Now, perhaps, you can imagine a little bit what life was like for Helen Keller, who became one of the most educated and active women who ever lived in spite of those handicaps. ■

ALSO READ: BRAILLE, HEARING, SIGHT, SPECIAL EDUCATION.

KENNEDY, JOHN FITZGER-ALD (1917–1963) "My fellow Americans," said John F. Kennedy in his address when he was inaugurated President of the United States, "ask not what your country can do for you; ask what you can do for your country." All that needed to be done could not be accomplished in a hundred days, not even in a thousand, he said, "But let us begin."

John F. Kennedy was born in Brookline, Massachusetts, on May 29, 1917. He was one of four boys, the second oldest son, in a family of nine children. His father, Joseph Kennedy, was a wealthy businessman who later served as ambassador to Great Britain.

During World War II, John joined the U.S. Navy. He was commander of a patrol torpedo boat (PT boat) in the South Pacific. One night, his boat was rammed by a Japanese destroyer. Lieutenant Kennedy was later awarded various medals for the courage he showed in saving the lives of some members of his crew.

A year after his discharge from the Navy, he went into politics. At the age of 29, he was elected to the U.S. House of Representatives as a congressman from Massachusetts. In 1952, he was elected to the Senate, but while serving as a senator, he had to have an operation on his back. He lived through the operation, but he was never again completely free of pain. While recovering, he wrote *Profiles in Courage*, a collection of biographies about earlier lawmakers who had shown great courage. This book won the Pulitzer Prize in 1956.

Senator Kennedy was nominated for President by the Democratic Party in 1960. In his campaign, Kennedy promised to open up for America a "New Frontier"—a program of new ideas to improve the lives of all Americans. Millions of Americans watched a series of televised debates between Kennedy and his Republican opponent, Richard Milhous Nixon. He defeated Nixon in a close election.

In his first year as President, Kennedy worked for laws to help the poor people of America with better housing, more relief (money for people

JOHN FITZGERALD KENNEDY
THIRTY-FIFTH PRESIDENT JANUARY 21, 1961—NOVEMBER 22, 1963

Born: May 29, 1917, Brookline, Massachusetts
Parents: Joseph Patrick and Rose Fitzgerald Kennedy
Education: Harvard University, Cambridge, Mass.
Religion: Roman Catholic
Occupation: Author and legislator
Political Party: Democratic
State Represented: Massachusetts
Married: 1953 to Jacqueline Lee Bouvier (born 1929)
Children: 1 daughter; 2 sons (one died in infancy)
Died: November 22, 1963, Dallas, Texas
Buried: Arlington National Cemetery, Arlington, Va.

unable to work), and a higher minimum hourly wage (the smallest amount of money a company is allowed to pay a worker). Kennedy founded the U.S. Peace Corps in 1961. The Peace Corps sends many young Americans to work with the people of underdeveloped countries. Kennedy also encouraged the development of the U.S. space program. During the early 1960's, the civil rights movement was organizing to protest discrimination against black people in the United States. Kennedy tried to persuade Congress to pass a civil rights law to give black people equal rights. But he was unable to get support in Congress.

Kennedy, his wife Jacqueline, and their two children, Caroline and John, Jr., brought the life and gaiety of a young family to the White House. Jacqueline Kennedy had many of the rooms in the White House furnished with historical furniture of the 1700's and 1800's. The Kennedys invited famous artists, musicians, and writers to the White House and encouraged their work.

Kennedy worked for a more friendly relationship between the United States and the Soviet Union. An attitude of suspicion and hostility, called the "Cold War," had existed between the two countries since the end of World War II. Kennedy and the Soviet premier, Nikita Khrushchev, met to discuss common problems. But in 1961, the United States backed an invasion of the island of Cuba, which had recently been taken over by a Communist government. The invasion was a failure. The following year, the Russians began to build missile bases in Cuba. The United States told the Soviet Union to remove the missile bases or risk starting a war. The Russians finally removed the weapons. In 1963, the United States, the Soviet Union, and Great Britain signed a treaty saying that they would not test nuclear weapons in the air or under the water.

On November 22, 1963, President Kennedy was assassinated in Dallas, Texas. The whole world mourned for the young President who was killed before his work was completed. The man accused of shooting the President, Lee Harvey Oswald, was shot by a man named Jack Ruby before he could be tried. Kennedy was succeeded by his Vice-President, Lyndon Baines Johnson. Johnson persuaded Congress to pass several laws that Kennedy had failed to have passed, including the Civil Rights Bill of 1964.

Millions have visited Kennedy's grave, over which an "eternal flame" burns, in Arlington National Cemetery. In 1971, the John F. Kennedy Center for the Performing Arts was opened in Washington, D.C., as an active memorial to him.

ALSO READ: ASSASSINATION; CAPE CANAVERAL; CIVIL RIGHTS MOVEMENT; CUBA; JOHNSON, LYNDON BAINES; KHRUSHCHEV, NIKITA; NIXON, RICHARD MILHOUS; PEACE CORPS.

KENNEDY, ROBERT FITZGERALD (1925–1968)

Robert Kennedy, the younger brother of President John F. Kennedy, also had a distinguished career in government. "Bobby" Kennedy played a big part in the success of his brother's Presidential campaign in 1960.

Robert Kennedy was appointed by his brother to be U.S. Attorney General, and was a close adviser to the President on many important matters concerning home and foreign affairs. As Attorney General, he took a determined stand in the government's fight against organized crime, and he also won much support for his backing of the civil rights movement. In 1961 Kennedy sent federal marshals to Montgomery, Alabama, to protect Martin Luther King, Jr., and 1,200 civil rights supporters who were being threatened by a hostile mob.

John Kennedy's book, *Profiles in Courage*, is published in an edition especially for young readers. Your city library may have a copy.

▲ *Robert F. Kennedy served as Attorney General during the Presidency of his brother John F. Kennedy. With the promise of a brilliant political career ahead of him, Robert Kennedy was assassinated in 1968.*

Mammoth Cave in Kentucky is one of the world's wonders. It has 300 miles (480 km) of explored passageways, 200-foot-high (60-m-high) chambers, and vast columns of stalagmites and stalactites. Visitors can take a boat ride on a river 360 feet (110 m) below ground.

The assassination of John Kennedy in November 1963 was a terrible shock to his brother, as it was to the whole world. Robert Kennedy stayed on as Attorney General until he resigned in September 1964. He was elected Senator from New York and became a critic of the Johnson administration. In 1968 he campaigned for the Democratic nomination for the Presidency and won five out of six early primary elections. But while campaigning in California, on June 5, 1968, he was shot and mortally wounded in a hotel in Los Angeles by an Arab immigrant named Sirhan Bishara Sirhan.

Robert Kennedy is buried in Arlington National Cemetery, near his brother President John Kennedy.

KENTUCKY The heartland of Kentucky is known for thoroughbred racehorses. It is the famous bluegrass region. Only in spring—usually in May—does the grass have a bluish tint. But blue or green, Kentucky bluegrass is excellent food for horses. Horse farms lie all around the city of Lexington. Racehorses are given the best of care in clean, white stables.

The Land Kentucky lies north of Tennessee. It is west of Virginia and West Virginia. Its northern boundary is formed by the Ohio River, which separates Kentucky from Ohio, Indiana, and Illinois. The Ohio River meets the Mississippi River near the western end of Kentucky. The Mississippi River separates Kentucky from Missouri. The Mississippi makes a sharp double curve along this border. It cuts off an area of about 10 square miles (25 sq. km) from the rest of Kentucky. To reach this area from the main part of Kentucky, you must go through a bit of either Missouri or Tennessee!

Kentucky is divided into three land regions—all very different. The first is the southeastern third of the state. It belongs to the Cumberland Plateau. Streams have cut narrow valleys through this highland. Steep, narrow hills separate the valleys. There are many coal mines here.

The second part stretches westward from the first. It covers all the rest of the state's southern part. Here is the Pennyroyal, or Pennyrile, Plateau. Its name comes from that of a fragrant wild plant found there. Parts of the plateau are hilly, but other parts are almost level. The plateau is good farming country. North of it is another big coal field.

The third part of Kentucky is separated from the second by the Knobs, a curving, knoblike range of hills. This third part is the bluegrass region, and has the best farmland. Crops, as well as horses, are raised here.

Kentucky has a good climate for farming. Summers are long and hot. There is usually enough rain. Winters are generally short.

History Many ancient Indian tribes lived in Kentucky. Graves, stone tools, and bits of pottery found here show us where their villages once stood. Some of these Indians lived in caves.

White people were relatively late in settling Kentucky. The Appalachian Mountains formed a natural barrier between this region and the colonies on the East Coast. Only a few French and English explorers entered it be-

▼ *Canoeists enjoy the outdoors near the Cumberland Falls, Kentucky.*

ILLINOIS

INDIANA

OHIO

Cincinnati

Covington

Ohio

Ashland   Huntington

W. VA

Morehead

Kentucky

BLUEGRASS
REGION

Louisville

★ Frankfort

Lexington

Fort Knox

Winchester

Ohio

Henderson

Owensboro

Radcliff

Danville

Richmond

Pikeville

Elizabethtown

Berea

PLATEAU

Hazard

Rough
River
Lake

Madisonville

Green

MAMMOTH
CAVE N.P.

Somerset

CUMBERLAND

APPALACHIAN MTS.

MO.

Tennessee

Paducah

Lake
Barkley

Hopkinsville

Bowling
Green

Glasgow

Lake
Cumberland

Cumberland

Mayfield

PENNYROYAL PLATEAU

Dale
Hollow
Lake

Middlesboro

VIRGINIA

Kentucky
Lake

Mississippi

0   25   50
Miles

TENNESSEE

KENTUCKY

Capital
Frankfort (26,000 people)

Area
40,409 square miles (104,628
sq. km)
Rank: 37th

Population
3,726,000 people
Rank: 23rd

Statehood
June 1, 1792
(15th state admitted)

Principal river
Ohio River

Highest point
Big Black Mountain
4,150 feet (1,265 m)

Largest city
Louisville (290,000 people)

Motto
United we stand, divided we
fall.

Song
"My Old Kentucky Home"

Famous people
Muhammad Ali, Abraham
Lincoln, Loretta Lynn, Diane
Sawyer, Victor Mature,
Jefferson Davis

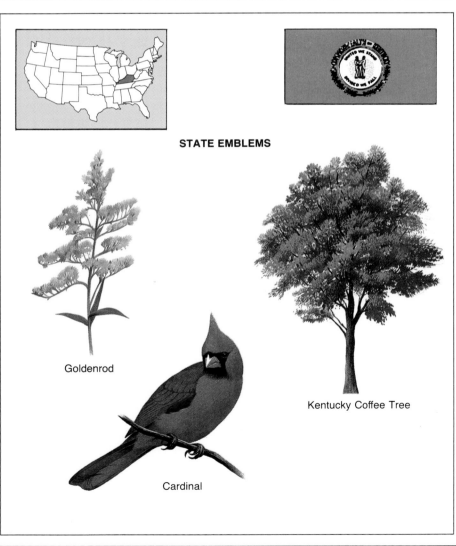

STATE EMBLEMS

Goldenrod

Cardinal

Kentucky Coffee Tree

▲ *The Kentucky landscape is dotted with some fine old homes. "My Old Kentucky Home," near Bardstown, was built about 1795. People dressed in the fashions of the time prepare to welcome visitors.*

▶ *Visitors explore the frozen Niagara section of Mammoth Cave, the largest single cave in the world. The cave is the most spectacular sight in Mammoth Cave National Park, a 50,000-acre (20,235-hectare) wonderland in central Kentucky.*

fore 1750. In that year, five Virginians, led by Dr. Thomas Walker, reached it. They followed an Indian trail, which took them through a pass of the Appalachians into Kentucky. Dr. Walker named the pass Cumberland Gap, in honor of the Duke of Cumberland.

The British government did not want American colonists to move west. It wanted the land beyond the Appalachian Mountains left to the Shawnees, Wyandottes, Cherokees, and other Indians. They hoped this would prevent more Indian wars. Also, Indian hunters would always be able to get the furs that the English wanted. But it was impossible to hold back the frontier people. James Harrod, Daniel Boone, and other pioneer scouts hunted and explored in Kentucky. They liked the bluegrass region especially. Boone called it "a second paradise." Harrod led a group of pioneers to central Kentucky in 1774. They founded Harrodsburg. The next year Daniel Boone and his friends began work on Boonesborough. These were the first two settlements in Kentucky.

During the American Revolution, Kentucky settlers fought Indians who were on the British side. Sometimes British soldiers helped the tribes in battle. The last big Indian fight on Kentucky soil took place in 1782. Kentucky became a state ten years later. It was the first state west of the Appalachians. Thousands of settlers

came there by wagon on the Wilderness Road, which led through the Cumberland Gap. Others floated down the Ohio River in clumsy flatboats. The population of Kentucky grew quickly.

Slavery was legal in Kentucky. But many of the state's people believed it was wrong. When the Civil War began, the state did not leave the Union, but soldiers from Kentucky joined both the Northern and Southern armies.

The state's most valuable crop has always been tobacco. For a time, most of Kentucky's money came from this one crop. When tobacco didn't sell very well, farmers had little money. The whole state suffered.

The state was helped by the growth of manufacturing. Kentucky is rich in bituminous (soft) coal. Seventy or eighty years ago, coal was the fuel used for almost all manufacturing, transportation, and heating. Kentucky mine owners grew rich, but many Kentuckians who worked as miners were very poorly paid. By the 1940's, however, their wages were much higher. But two new fuels—oil and natural gas—were taking business away from the coal miners. Today, unemployment and poverty are still serious problems in the coal fields of Kentucky.

Kentuckians at Work Manufacturing is the leading industry in Kentucky today. Most of it is done along the Ohio River. The largest industrial center is the city of Louisville. Electrical machinery, processed foods and drinks, chemicals, and tobacco products are the state's major manufactured goods. Kentucky is the nation's leading producer of whiskey, having distilleries in many cities.

Mining is the state's second most important industry. There are large, valuable deposits of coal, petroleum, natural gas, and fluorite (a mineral used in making steel and glass). Kentucky mines more tons of coal each year than any other state.

Agriculture produces almost as much income as mining does. Burley tobacco and dark tobacco are the main crops. Kentucky grows more tobacco than any other state except North Carolina. Corn, hay, soybeans, and fruits are also valuable crops. Farmers throughout the state also raise cattle, hogs, sheep, and poultry.

Among Kentucky's natural wonders is Mammoth Cave. It is one of the largest caves on Earth. About 300 miles (480 km) of its underground passages have been explored. Visitors can take guided trips through the cave. Historical places attract thousands of tourists to Kentucky. They can see, among other things, the birthplaces of Abraham Lincoln and Jefferson Davis, presidents of the North and the South during the Civil War. Both men were born in Kentucky log cabins.

ALSO READ: BOONE, DANIEL; WILDERNESS ROAD.

KENYA The Republic of Kenya is one of the busiest tourist centers of East Africa. Many wild animals of Africa can be seen in Kenya in protected areas called *game preserves*. Tourists from all over the world travel on *safaris* (expeditions) into these vast wildlife reserves to photograph them.

Kenya is about the size of the state of Texas. The republic of Somalia and the Indian Ocean form the country's eastern boundary. Tanzania lies to the south, and Uganda forms the western boundary. The Sudan and Ethiopia are its northern neighbors. (See the map with the article on AFRICA.)

In Kenya, the land rises gently inland from the palm-fringed beaches and the bustling port of Mombasa. The modern capital of Nairobi is about a mile (1.6 km) above sea level in the green, rolling highlands of central Kenya. The climate in the highlands is cool and temperate compared to the tropical heat of the coast. The snowcapped peak of 17,058-foot-high (5,199-m-high) Mount Kenya, the highest mountain in the country, is located about 100 miles (160 km) northeast of Nairobi. Cutting through the highlands from north to south is the Great Rift Valley. This huge valley stretches from Syria in the north through the Red Sea and East Africa to Mozambique. In northern Kenya, Lake Turkana lies in the valley. To the east of the valley is a hot, dry region of barren mountains and scrub-covered plains.

Among the tribes in Kenya are the Kikuyu, Luo, Baluhya, Kamba, and Masai. Some of the tall, thin Masai people still dress in blankets and skins and wear colorful jewelry. They tend herds of cows. Kikuyu people and most other Kenyans make their living by farming. Coffee, corn, wheat, and tea are the principal crops grown in the highlands. Sugar, cashew nuts, and cotton are grown on the coastal plains. Agricultural products are

▲ *Nairobi, the capital of Kenya, is today a busy modern city.*

According to United Nations figures, the highest birthrate for any country in any year was for Kenya in 1980. The figure was 54 babies for every 1,000 inhabitants. The world figure is about 27.

KENYA

Capital City: Nairobi (960,000 people).
Area: 224,961 square miles (582,604 sq. km).
Population: 23,700,000.
Government: One-party republic.
Natural Resources: Soda ash.
Export Products: Coffee, tea, petroleum products.
Unit of Money: Kenya shilling.
Official Languages: English, Swahili.

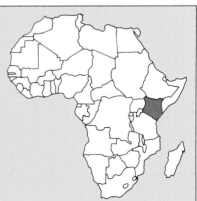

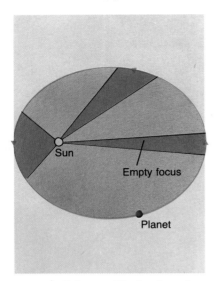

▲ *Johannes Kepler showed that the planets follow elliptical paths around the sun. An ellipse has two points, or "focuses," within it. The sun is situated at one focus; the other is empty.*

▼ *Nikita Khrushchev (right) and Fidel Castro of Cuba cemented the close ties between their two countries after the Cuban revolution of 1959.*

processed for export and goods are manufactured for the Kenyan people. Tourism is a major source of income.

Arabian merchants set up trading posts on the Kenyan coast in the A.D. 600's. They traded in slaves and ivory. Hundreds of years later, Portuguese, Indian, and British traders also settled in the region. In 1895, the British took over the coast and began to develop the interior. The whole region became a colony of Great Britain. White settlers took over farmland that belonged to the Kikuyu people. In the 1950's, some Kikuyus began an armed movement, called the Mau Mau, to win independence from the British.

Kenya finally became independent in 1963 and a republic in 1964. Jomo Kenyatta, who had been imprisoned as leader of the Mau Mau, became president. When he died in 1978, Vice-President Daniel Arap Moi became president. He was elected in 1979 and again in 1983.

ALSO READ: AFRICA.

KEPLER, JOHANNES (1571–1630)

Johannes Kepler was born in Weil der Stadt, Wurttemberg, Germany. At the age of three he caught smallpox, which left him with poor eyesight and crippled hands. Kepler trained as a minister but was soon recognized as a brilliant mathematician. He became interested in astronomy and astrology.

Kepler went to work with Tycho Brahe, a brilliantly accurate observer of the night skies—even though the telescope had yet to be invented. When Tycho died in 1601 he left Kepler his records of observations.

By this time the ideas of Nicolaus Copernicus were widely known. Copernicus said that the planets moved in circular paths around the sun. But this did not fit in with the observations of other astronomers, including Kepler. Using Tycho's observations of Mars, he tried to work out the path of the planet. After many years he proved that the planet orbited the sun in an elliptical path. (An ellipse is like a flattened circle.) He then worked out many other important laws ("rules") about the planets' orbits. These later formed the groundwork for Sir Isaac Newton's discovery of universal gravitation.

ALSO READ: ASTRONOMY; BRAHE, TYCHO; COPERNICUS, NICOLAUS; GRAVITY AND GRAVITATION; NEWTON, ISAAC; ORBIT.

KEROSENE

Kerosene is a colorless oil, heavier than gasoline and lighter than diesel fuel. It is made from petroleum but has been obtained from wood, oil shale, and coal. Kerosene, spelled *kerosine* in the oil industry, is sometimes called *coal oil*.

The main use of kerosene is as a fuel for jet aircraft. Some tractors and other farm machinery run on kerosene, which is also used in insecticides, stoves, and lamps.

ALSO READ: FUEL, PETROLEUM.

KEY, FRANCIS SCOTT see STAR-SPANGLED BANNER.

KHMER REPUBLIC see KAMPUCHEA.

KHRUSHCHEV, NIKITA (1894–1971)

The man who was premier and head of the Communist Party of the Soviet Union from 1958 to 1964 was the son of a poor coal miner. Throughout his career, Nikita Sergeyevich Khrushchev worked to give the Russian people an easier and more prosperous way of life. He always believed in Communism as the most important political force in the world. He often urged that Communist ideals should be spread by peaceful means and nations should live together in peace.

Nikita Khrushchev was born in the village of Kalinovka in southwest Russia. At the age of 15, he went to work in the coal mines. He fought in the Russian civil war (1918–1920), in which the Bolsheviks (Communists) established themselves as rulers of the new Soviet Union. By 1935, he was head of the Communist Party in Moscow. Four years later, he was named a member of the Politburo, the top committee in the Communist Party.

The Soviet dictator, Joseph Stalin, died in 1953. Khrushchev became premier in 1958 after a fierce struggle for power among the top officials in the government. The Russian people had suffered terrible restrictions under Stalin's dictatorship. Khrushchev gave the people more freedom and set up programs to give them a better standard of living. He made this change in policy more dramatic by openly accusing Stalin of having committed crimes against the Russian people. Khrushchev encouraged the growth of industry and technology in the Soviet Union.

Under Khrushchev's rule, the terror of Stalin's government was relaxed. The people in countries under Soviet domination began to demand greater freedom. Khrushchev at first gave in to their demands, but a major revolt that broke out in Hungary in 1956 was mercilessly repressed.

The "Cold War" had existed between the Soviet Union and the United States since the end of World War II. Khrushchev now spoke of the need for peace and friendship between the two powers. But in 1962, he brought the two countries to the brink of war by setting up missile bases on the island of Cuba. War was averted only when President John F. Kennedy forced Khrushchev to withdraw the missiles. A quarrel also developed between Russia and China.

By the 1960's, other top members of the Soviet government were seriously concerned about the quarrel with China. They felt that Khrushchev had been weak in his dealings with the West. Khrushchev's development programs in the Soviet Union had not been highly successful, and he was losing popularity with the people. On October 14, 1964, the Soviet Communist Party removed Khrushchev as leader of the Soviet government. He lived in retirement until his death in 1971.

ALSO READ: KENNEDY, JOHN FITZGERALD; SOVIET UNION.

KIDD, CAPTAIN see PIRATES AND PRIVATEERS.

KIDNEY The kidneys are two purplish-red, bean-shaped organs, which rid the body of liquid waste called *urine*.

There is one kidney on each side of your backbone, just above the small of your back. A human kidney is about 4½ inches (11.5 cm) long, 2 inches (5 cm) wide, and 1½ inches (4 cm) thick.

A kidney has two main parts, an outer *cortex* and an inner *medulla*. Blood enters a kidney through an artery that divides into branches within the medulla. These branches go to the cortex, where they further divide into tiny knots of capillaries called *glomeruli*. Surrounding the glomeruli are tiny kidney *tubules*. Each tubule, along with a single glomerulus, forms what is called a *nephron*. Each kidney contains thousands of nephrons. The nephrons separate waste matter from plasma, the liquid part of the blood. The wastes, together with a small amount of water in which they are dissolved, make up urine. The blood, cleaned of wastes, goes out of the kidney through a vein.

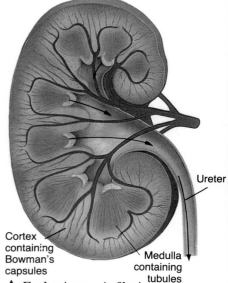

Cortex containing Bowman's capsules

Ureter

Medulla containing tubules

▲ *Each microscopic filtering unit inside a kidney has a cup-shaped structure called a Bowman's capsule. Water and dissolved chemicals pass from the blood into the capsule. Useful substances are taken back into the blood from the tubules. Urine, containing waste chemicals, is carried to the bladder through the ureter.*

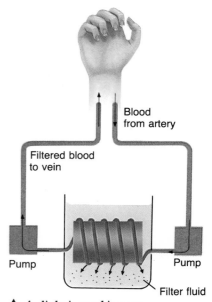

Blood from artery

Filtered blood to vein

Pump

Pump

Filter fluid

▲ *A dialysis machine can take the place of the kidneys. Blood from the patient is pumped over a thin membrane that allows water and waste chemicals to pass through.*

Your kidneys filter about 40 gallons (150 liters) of fluid each day. The bladder can hold up to three-fourths of a pint (400 cc) of liquid.

Nearly one-fifth of the blood pumped by the heart goes through the kidneys. A person can survive without any kidneys for only two or three weeks.

Urine goes from a nephron to a tube called a *collecting tubule*. Urine from many collecting tubules flows down from each kidney through a tube called a ureter. The two ureters empty into the *urinary bladder*.

A kidney may become diseased and fail to work. If this happens to both kidneys, wastes collect in the blood, and this eventually causes death. It is now possible to help a person whose kidneys do not function. A healthy kidney, from another person, may be *transplanted*, or surgically attached in place of a diseased kidney. When the donor and patient are closely related, the success of the transplant is more likely than when they are unrelated.

If there is no one from whom to get a kidney, a person with kidney failure can be kept alive by use of a *dialysis machine*. A tube is put into an artery in the sick person's arm, and another tube is put into a vein in the arm. His or her blood flows from the artery into the machine and is cleaned of wastes. The purified blood then returns to the body through the vein. This treatment usually is needed at least twice a week.

ALSO READ: BLOOD, DIGESTION.

KINDERGARTEN see SCHOOL.

KING, MARTIN LUTHER, JR. (1929–1968) "I have a dream that one day this nation will rise up and live out the true meaning of its creed: 'We hold these truths to be self-evident, that all men are created equal.'" These words were spoken by Martin Luther King, Jr. in 1963. He was speaking to a crowd of more than 200,000 people who had come to Washington, D.C. to march for civil rights for all people. Dr. King believed in equal and fair laws and opportunities for all people, no matter what their race, their religion, or what country they come from. Dr. King

worked all his life to make this dream of equality come true.

Martin Luther King, Jr., was born in Atlanta, Georgia. He was the son of a Baptist minister and became a Baptist minister himself in 1947. He graduated from Morehouse College in 1948, received his Bachelor of Divinity degree (B.D.) from Crozer Theological Seminary in 1951 and his Doctor of Philosophy degree (Ph.D.) from Boston University in 1955. In 1954, he became pastor of a church in Montgomery, Alabama.

Dr. King first became known in the civil rights movement during the 1950's. In 1955, he led the black citizens of Montgomery in a peaceful *boycott* of the city buses. During a boycott, people refuse to use certain things, buy certain products, or deal with certain companies. The black people of Montgomery refused to ride the city's buses because blacks were always made to sit in the back. The boycott succeeded. The bus company finally agreed to let the blacks sit in any seats on a Montgomery bus.

Dr. King helped organize the Southern Christian Leadership Conference (SCLC) in 1957. The purpose of this organization was to fight for civil rights and against racial discrimination. As president of the SCLC, Dr. King led many marches against racial discrimination. These marches made people see the injustice of discrimination and encouraged lawmakers and government officials to do something to correct it.

Dr. King preached *nonviolence* throughout his life. His idea of nonviolence was simple—changes must be made without fighting and without damaging other people's rights. King's work was largely responsible for the passage of the Civil Rights Act of 1964 and the Voting Rights Act of 1965. In 1964, Dr. King received the Nobel peace prize. He gave the prize money—more than 70,000 dollars—to the civil rights movement.

▲ *Dr. Martin Luther King, who worked all his life for civil rights for all people, regardless of race, religion, or nationality.*

Dr. King worked hard for equal school opportunities for both black and white children. In most areas of the country, black people could not buy or rent homes in certain white neighborhoods. Dr. King led marches in Chicago and other cities to protest racial discrimination in housing. Dr. King also fought against job discrimination. Companies often would not not hire black persons—even if they were qualified for the job—simply because they were black. Many businesses now advertise that they are "equal opportunity employers." This means that they no longer pay attention to a person's race, but hire people on the basis of their qualifications, and promote people on the basis of their abilities. These and many more changes have taken place through the efforts and bravery of Dr. King, his followers, and other workers for civil rights.

Although Dr. King advocated nonviolence, he died a violent death. On April 4, 1968, in Memphis, Tennessee, Dr. King was shot and killed by James Earl Ray, an escaped convict. In memory of Dr. King, his birthday, January 15, is now celebrated as a federal holiday.

ALSO READ: BLACK AMERICANS, CIVIL RIGHTS, CIVIL RIGHTS MOVEMENT.

KING, W. L. MACKENZIE (1874–1950) William Lyon Mackenzie King was prime minister of Canada for a longer period than anyone else in Canadian history. Born in Ontario in 1874, he was named after his grandfather, who had led an unsuccessful rebellion against the British in Canada in 1837.

Mackenzie King studied at the University of Toronto, the University of Chicago, and Harvard University. The social work he did in Chicago inspired him to investigate and expose unhealthy and unfair working conditions in Toronto. He helped to estab-lish a Department of Labour in Canada and later served as Minister of Labour.

Mackenzie King was chosen as the leader of the Liberal Party in 1919. His party won the election of 1921, and he became prime minister. Except for a brief period in 1926 and the five years from 1930 to 1935, Mackenzie King served in that office until his retirement in 1948.

He began a national social security program in Canada by establishing old-age pensions (salaries for retired people). Mackenzie King helped to unify his country by treating both English- and French-speaking Canadians fairly.

ALSO READ: CANADA, COMMONWEALTH OF NATIONS, PRIME MINISTER.

KINGS AND QUEENS A king is a man who rules a country for life, usually by inheriting the position. A queen is either the wife of a king or a woman who rules a country herself. Such a ruler—male or female—is called a *monarch*. The monarch's wife or husband is called a *consort*. Monarchs and their families are called

▲ *Mackenzie King, former Canadian prime minister, votes in an election.*

▼ *King Darius of Persia flees in his chariot from the forces of Alexander the Great in the Battle of Issus in 333 B.C.*

royalty. The monarch rules until he or she dies, or steps down (abdicates).

A monarch usually takes office in an elaborate ceremony called a *coronation*. At this ceremony the crown—the symbol of power—is placed upon the monarch's head.

The eldest son of a king usually becomes king when his father dies. If the king has no sons, his oldest daughter becomes queen after his death. Queen Elizabeth II became the monarch of Great Britain after her father, King George VI, died in 1952. When a monarch has no children, a brother or another close relation may succeed to the throne.

Forty-five centuries ago in the land called Mesopotamia (now Iraq), Sumerian kings ruled city-states. To lead an attack against another city-state, the king would put on his golden helmet, climb into his war chariot, and order his soldiers, who were armed with lances and bows and arrows, to follow him into battle.

The ancient Babylonians, who came to power in Mesopotamia after the Sumerians, had a strange custom. At the time of the New Year, the real king would "retire" for a day to get out of the sight of gods who might be angry with him. The Babylonians then chose a prisoner or a slave to be "king-for-a-day." A festival was held, with music and games. When the day ended, the real king returned, and the substitute king was killed.

The ancient Egyptian kings were called *pharaohs*. The Egyptians believed that their pharaohs were gods. The pharaohs ordered great pyramids built as burial places for themselves. The pharaoh was almost always a man. But Queen Hatshepsut broke this tradition about 1490 B.C., when she proclaimed herself pharaoh. She assumed all the titles and badges of office and even wore a false beard. She ruled for about 20 years.

Alexander the Great was an important king during the time when ancient Greece was powerful. He be-

▲ *A woodcut showing the execution of Charles I of England in 1649. The monarchy was not restored until 1660.*

came King of Macedonia, a land to the north of Greece, when he was 20 years old. Before he died at the age of 33, he had conquered much of the land surrounding the eastern end of the Mediterranean Sea, as well as the vast Persian Empire. Alexander brought Greek civilization to all these regions. He was one of the most successful military commanders of all times.

Julius Caesar was a Roman statesman and general. Although he ruled the Roman Empire like a king, Caesar took the title of *dictator* instead. Julius Caesar was so powerful that the Roman emperors who followed him all took the title "Caesar." The leader of the Russian Empire before World War I was called a *czar*, from the word *Caesar*. And the emperors of the Holy Roman Empire, Austria, and Germany were called *kaisers*.

Kings of the Middle Ages Many stories are told of the great King Arthur. A king named Arthurius did rule in western England in the Middle Ages. But storytellers made up the fascinating tales of the adventures of Arthur and his Knights of the Round Table.

A famous real king of the Middle Ages was Charlemagne. He extended his empire from what is now France

▲ *Louis XIV of France was an "absolute" ruler whose word was all-powerful. At that time, many people believed that kings were given "divine right" to rule by God.*

to include most of western Europe. Charlemagne was a wise and hard-working king. He wanted his people to become educated, so he established schools where both rich and poor could study.

In 1215, England began to limit the power of kings. A group of noblemen forced King John to sign a document that promised the noblemen certain rights. This document was called the *Magna Carta*. The king at the same time agreed that all freemen had definite legal rights that no king could take away from them. Some ideas from the Magna Carta are found in democratic constitutions to this day.

Modern Kings Over the centuries, the power of kings has declined. Republics have taken the place of many kingdoms. The people elect legislatures to make laws. Today, almost no king can do just as he wishes. Most modern kings *reign* (hold office), but they do not rule over the people.

In Britain, Queen Elizabeth II reigns, but Parliament and the prime minister govern. The British people feel that their king or queen gives them an important symbol of unity. They enjoy the ceremonies associated with the royal family. In Europe, the countries of Norway, Sweden, Denmark, Belgium, and the Netherlands each have a king or a queen. But a prime minister and a legislature make the laws that govern each country.

In Morocco, a country in Africa, King Hassan II is trying to use his power to build up his nation. Japan adopted a democratic constitution after being defeated in World War II, but it kept its emperor. Today, the emperor of Japan attends ceremonial functions and lives in the Imperial Palace in Tokyo.

In Ethiopia, Emperor Haile Selassie reigned for 58 years, until in 1974 he was deposed by a military coup. His son was a figurehead king until the monarchy was abolished the next year. In 1975, the 300-year monarchy

in Sikkim was also abolished when voters approved the uniting of Sikkim with India and ousted the king. Sikkim had been ruled by the maharajah and his maharani (queen) like a kingdom of the Middle Ages.

For further information on:
Ancient Kings, *see* ALARIC; ALEXANDER THE GREAT; CAESAR, JULIUS; NERO.
Kings, *see* ALFRED THE GREAT; ARTHUR, KING; BRUCE, ROBERT; CANUTE, KING; CHARLEMAGNE; CHARLES, HOLY ROMAN EMPERORS; CHARLES, KINGS OF ENGLAND; CHARLES, KINGS OF FRANCE; CHARLES MARTEL; EDWARD, KINGS OF ENGLAND; EDWARD THE CONFESSOR; FRANCIS, KINGS OF FRANCE; GENGHIS KHAN; HENRY, HOLY ROMAN EMPERORS; HENRY, KINGS OF ENGLAND; HENRY, KINGS OF FRANCE; ISABELLA AND FERDINAND; JAMES, KINGS OF ENGLAND; JOHN, KING OF ENGLAND; LOUIS, KINGS OF FRANCE; NICHOLAS, CZARS OF RUSSIA; PHILIP, KINGS OF FRANCE; PHILIP, KINGS OF SPAIN; WILLIAM, KINGS OF ENGLAND; WILLIAM AND MARY.
Queens, *see* ANNE; CLEOPATRA; ELEANOR OF AQUITAINE; ELIZABETH I; ELIZABETH II; GREY, LADY JANE; LILIUOKALANI, LYDIA; MARY, QUEEN OF SCOTS; MARY, QUEENS OF ENGLAND.

▲ *Queen Elizabeth II sits enthroned in the House of Lords for the traditional opening of Parliament. Real power is in the hands of Parliament and the prime minister.*

▲ *Gustavus Adolphus, King of Sweden 1611–32, who gained much territory for his country with sweeping military victories during the Thirty Years' War. He was killed in battle.*

▲ *Rudyard Kipling, who wrote sympathetically about India under British rule.*

The inventor of the telephone, Alexander Graham Bell, made a kite large enough to lift a lieutenant of the United States Army to a height of 175 feet (53 m).

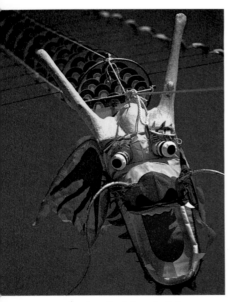

▲ *A colorful and elaborate Chinese kite in the form of a dragon.*

KIPLING, RUDYARD (1865–1936)

The British writer, Rudyard Kipling, was born in Bombay, India. India was part of the British Empire at the time. Kipling glorified the empire in many of his works, but he also wrote with sympathetic understanding about the people and stories of India.

Kipling was sent to England to be educated when he was only six. At the age of 17, he returned to India and went to work as a newspaper reporter. He began to write the short stories that made him famous. Kipling was a brilliant, imaginative storyteller. He vividly described the excitement and atmosphere of the places in his stories. His first two collections of stories, *Soldiers Three* and *Plain Tales from the Hills*, were very successful. Kipling returned to England in 1889. He wrote more stories and a popular series of verses, *Barrack-Room Ballads*, about the life of British soldiers in India. In 1892, he married an American girl and went to live in Vermont. But he later returned to England and settled.

He wrote several successful novels, including *Kim*, about the adventures of an orphan boy in India, and *Captains Courageous*, about a spoiled rich boy who changes his ways after spending some time with deep-sea fishermen on a ship. The adventures of Mowgli, a boy brought up by animals, are described in Kipling's two *Jungle Books*. Other books that he wrote for children are *Puck of Pook's Hill* and the *Just So Stories*.

ALSO READ: CHILDREN'S LITERATURE.

KIRIBATI
see MICRONESIA; PACIFIC ISLANDS.

KITE
A kite is a lightweight device built to be flown in the wind at the end of a string. It usually has a wooden or plastic frame, over which paper or cloth is stretched. Kites are especially popular in Asia. In Korea, people fly kites on the first few days of the new year as a kind of celebration. In Japan, kite flying is an important part of the boys' festival that is held each May 5. In China, the ninth day of the ninth month is celebrated as Kites' Day. At these special "kite celebrations," hundreds and thousands of kites are flown. They are made in all shapes, colors, and sizes. Some are shaped like fish, dragons, butterflies, or birds. All of them are very bright and colorful.

Most kite fans fly their kites just for fun, but serious kitefliers enter tournaments. These contests are conducted under the rules of the International Kitefliers Association.

Kites are used for practical purposes, too. The U.S. Weather Bureau used kites to gather information about winds and weather. Some of the kites used in this work carry scientific instruments and fly higher than 20,000 feet (6,000 m).

The *flat kite* is the simplest and most popular kite. The *box kite* is another common type. Today special *stunt kites*, made to dive and swoop in the sky, are also very popular.

■ LEARN BY DOING

A simple kite can be made with two crossed pieces of light wood glued to a sheet of paper or thin plastic. Then, all that's needed is a cloth tail, for balance, and a ball of cord—and, of course, a good wind.

To launch a kite, it's usually necessary to run into the wind. As the kite begins to rise, let out more line and give it some short tugs.

Do not fly a kite near trees or power lines. Also, you should not fly a kite in an area where there are low-flying aircraft. ■

KLONDIKE
see YUKON TERRITORY.